# The Children's Encyclopedia of
# OCEANS

Begin to discover the amazing underwater world

# The Children's Encyclopedia of
# OCEANS

Begin to discover the amazing underwater world

## PaRragon

Bath · New York · Singapore · Hong Kong · Cologne · Delhi · Melbourne

First published in 2010
Parragon
Queen Street House
4 Queen Street
Bath BA1 1HE, UK

Author: Sally Morgan
Consultant: John Weinberg
This edition produced by Tall Tree Ltd, London

British Library Cataloguing-in-Publication Data

A catalogue record for this book is
available from the British Library

ISBN 978-1-4454-0651-0

Printed in China

# Contents

# Introduction

Vast oceans cover much of the Earth's surface. They are home to millions of different animals – from the massive blue whale to tiny microscopic animals that float in the water.

This book takes you on a voyage of discovery through these enormous areas of water. You can learn about waves and tides. You will find out about animals that live along the coasts, on colourful coral reefs and in the open ocean – as well as the mysterious animals of the deep.

Finally, you can discover why the world's oceans are under threat and find out what is being done to protect them.

# The world's oceans

The Earth is often called the blue planet because more than two thirds of its surface is covered by water. Most of this water is found in the oceans. Oceans are huge areas of water that are many thousands of metres deep in places. The oceans are home to billions of animals and plants.

# Five oceans

There are five oceans. The largest is the Pacific Ocean, which stretches between North and South America, Australia and the eastern coast of Asia. The smallest is the Arctic Ocean, which surrounds the North Pole.

## Southern Ocean

The Southern Ocean surrounds Antarctica. Much of the Southern Ocean is over 4000 metres deep. It is a dangerous ocean with strong winds and massive icebergs.

## The oceans

All five of the world's oceans are connected. Smaller areas of water, called seas, are joined to some of the oceans. These include the Caribbean, Mediterranean and North Seas.

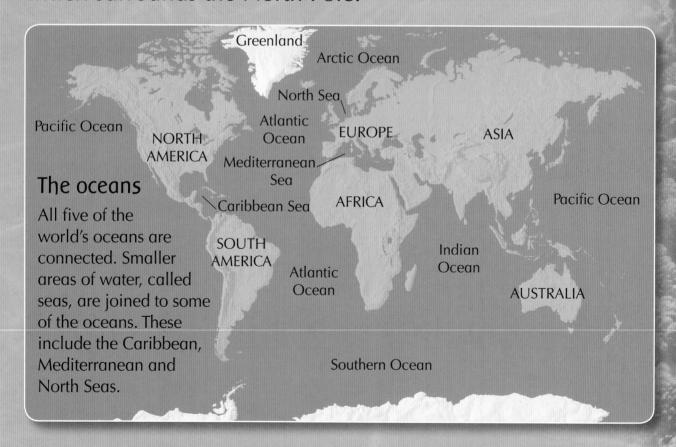

Greenland

Arctic Ocean

North Sea

Pacific Ocean

NORTH AMERICA

Atlantic Ocean

EUROPE

ASIA

Mediterranean Sea

Caribbean Sea

AFRICA

Pacific Ocean

SOUTH AMERICA

Atlantic Ocean

Indian Ocean

AUSTRALIA

Southern Ocean

## Ocean islands

Oceans are mostly wide, empty areas of water. Islands are scattered across the open oceans. These pieces of land rise up from under the water. Islands may cover large areas of land or just a few square kilometres.

A small island in the Indian Ocean.

## Coral reefs

Coral reefs are found off coasts and around islands in tropical parts of the world. Reefs are home to many kinds of fish and other colourful marine animals.

——— Coral reefs are built from the skeletons of tiny sea animals.

**DID YOU KNOW?**

The Pacific Ocean covers about 165 million square kilometres, that's over 15 times the size of the USA. The Arctic Ocean is just one and a half times the size of the USA.

# Exploring the oceans

The first boats were built more than 40,000 years ago from wood and animal skin. As boats became larger, people travelled away from the safety of the coast to explore the oceans.

## Ancient Egyptians

The Ancient Egyptians built wooden boats that they sailed around the Mediterranean Sea. They may have sailed over 1000 kilometres along the coast of Africa to present-day Ethiopia.

## Map making

The first maps of the world were drawn in the fifteenth century when much of the world was still unexplored. As explorers discovered new lands, the maps were updated.

## DID YOU KNOW?

In 1760, clock maker John Harrison invented the chronometer. It was a special clock that could keep time at sea, and enabled sailors to work out their east–west position.

This dhow is similar to the boats sailed by the Ancient Egyptians.

## Sir Walter Raleigh

In 1584, English explorer Sir Walter Raleigh sailed across the Atlantic Ocean and set up the first English settlement in North America. Many years later he explored the coast of South America.

## Astrolabe

This early navigational tool is called an astrolabe. Sailors used an astrolabe to work out how far north or south they were from the equator. To do this they needed to align the sighting rule in the middle of the disc with the Sun.

Sighting rule

Sixteenth-century astrolabe

## Captain Cook

James Cook was captain of the first European ship to land in Australia. His ship *Endeavour* left England in 1768 and sailed across the Pacific and around New Zealand before discovering Australia. He came ashore at Botany Bay, Australia in 1770.

Captain James Cook

A flat-bottomed hull allowed *Endeavour to* sail in shallow water.

13

## Breakers

When waves reach shallow water near a coast, they slow down and become taller. Finally, the top, or crest, of the wave topples over and crashes down onto the shore.

# Waves

Waves are created by wind blowing over the surface of the water. The stronger the wind, the bigger the waves. Waves travel across the ocean, just like ripples cross a pond.

## Tsunamis

Tsunamis are waves created by earthquakes under the ocean. By the time the waves reach the coast, they may be many metres tall. Powerful tsunamis can cause a lot of damage.

## Bow waves

Large waves form at the front, or bow, of a boat as it moves through water. During stormy weather waves break over the bow, and crash down on the deck.

## Surfing

Riding a surfboard on the crest of a wave is an exciting sport. Skilled surfers can twist and turn, jump in the air and ride their boards right under the wave as it rises up and curls.

**DID YOU KNOW?**

In 1993, a tsunami struck the island of Hokkaido, Japan. The waves were about 30 metres tall – that is as high as a 10-storey building.

In 2004, a tsunami caused a lot of damage to this village in Banda Aceh, Indonesia.

# Tides

Twice a day, the sea rises up a shore and then falls back again. High tide is when the sea reaches its highest point up a shore and low tide is when it is at its lowest point on the shore.

## Low tide

At low tide, the sea exposes the whole of the shore. In some places, the difference between high and low tides is great, but in others it is very small.

## The Sun and the Moon

The tides are caused by the pull of the Sun and the Moon. This pull is called gravity, and it pulls the Earth's oceans towards the Sun and Moon. This creates a bulge of water that produces the high tides. At the same time, there is less water in other parts of the ocean and this is what causes the low tides.

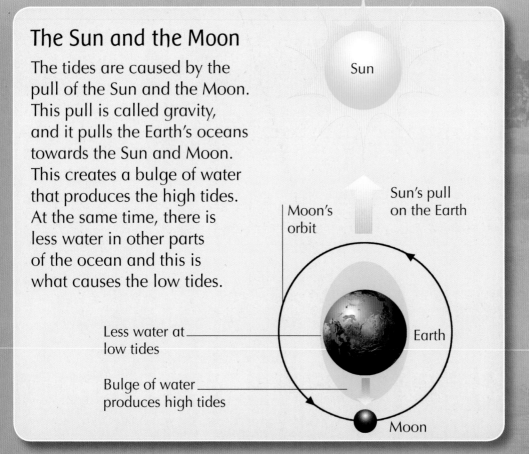

Sun

Moon's orbit

Sun's pull on the Earth

Less water at low tides

Earth

Bulge of water produces high tides

Moon

# Wading birds

Wading birds, such as oystercatchers and curlews (left), visit the coast at low tide to feed on small sea animals left uncovered by the tide. The birds poke in the mud or sand with their long bills, looking for worms and snails.

## Resting place

The exposed areas of the shore are home to many creatures. Animals such as seals can use the seashore as a place to rest and breed.

Male elephant seals have a nose that looks a bit like an elephant's trunk.

# Ocean currents

Oceans are never still. Winds blowing over the surface of the oceans create flows of water called currents. These currents travel around the world.

## Warm and cold currents

Currents of warm water flow from the equator towards the poles. Cold currents start in the Arctic and Antarctic and flow towards the equator.

## Mild winters

Tropical palm trees can grow in this southern part of Britain (below) because there is a warm current flowing along the coast. This makes mild winters, and snow and frost are rare.

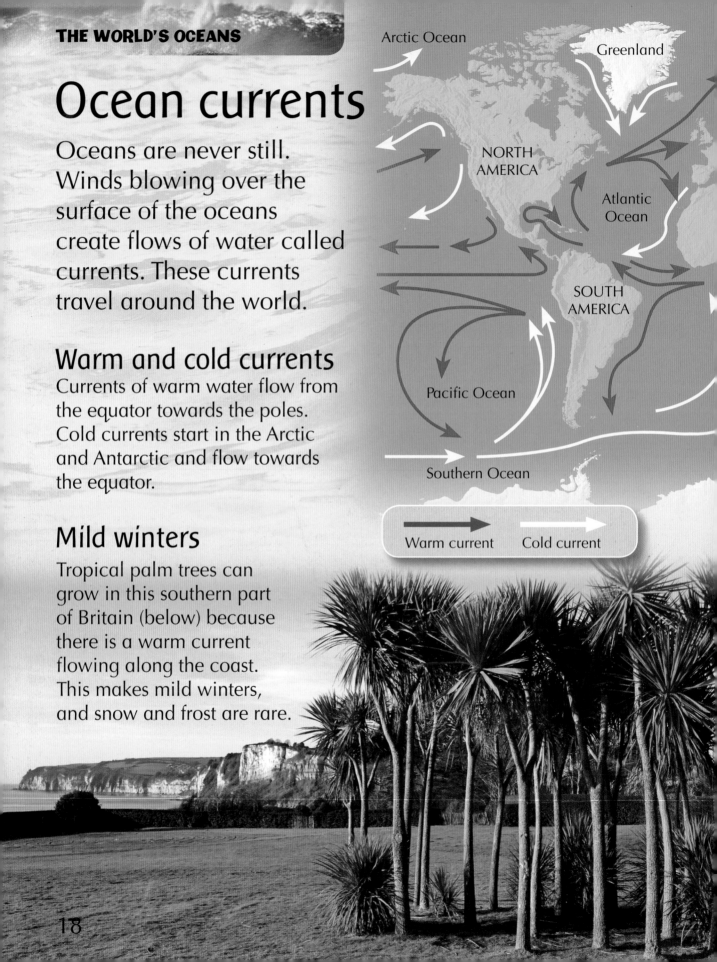

Arctic Ocean

Greenland

NORTH AMERICA

Atlantic Ocean

SOUTH AMERICA

Pacific Ocean

Southern Ocean

Warm current    Cold current

Arctic Ocean

ASIA

Pacific Ocean

Indian Ocean

AUSTRALIA

## Plankton

Sometimes, an ocean current brings up lots of food from the sea bed. Tiny plants and animals, called plankton, feed well and increase in number and form a plankton bloom. A plankton bloom can change the colour of the water and measure several hundred kilometres across.

Plankton

**DID YOU KNOW?**

The Gulf Stream is an ocean current that flows across the Atlantic Ocean from the Caribbean Sea to western Europe. It measures about 80–150 kilometres wide.

## Lots of fish

Some ocean currents are high in nutrients, and encourage plankton to grow. This attracts fish that feed on the plankton. The large numbers of fish attract predators such as seabirds.

A gull plucks a small fish from the water.

# Ocean weather

Oceans play an important role in the world's weather. Tropical storms, hurricanes and water spouts all form over water.

Storm clouds gather over the Caribbean Sea.

## Tropical storms

Rain falls most days in the regions nearest the equator, called the tropics. Storm clouds form off the coast during the day and bring a heavy downpour of rain at night.

The eye of the hurricane

## Hurricanes

Hurricanes are huge, spinning storms that form over warm water. Strong hurricane winds with speeds of up to 320 kilometres per hour can cause a lot of damage if they move on to land.

## Monsoon

Each year, winds from the Indian Ocean bring heavy rain to South-East Asia (right). These winds are called monsoons and they last several months. The monsoon season ends when the winds change direction and blow away from land.

Monsoon rains falling in India.

**DID YOU KNOW?**

On 27 July 2005, an amazing 94 centimetres of rain fell on Mumbai, India, in just 24 hours. This monsoon washed away thousands of homes, roads and railway tracks and killed more than 600 people.

## Water spout

A water spout is a spinning column of air and water that moves over water. It looks just like a miniature tornado. Although a water spout is not as dangerous as a tornado, it can damage small boats.

21

# Salt water

Seawater tastes very salty. This is because the water contains a lot of dissolved salt. Humans cannot drink seawater because it makes them ill. But animals that live in the sea have ways of coping with the high levels of salt.

## Salt pans

When salt water gathers in shallow ponds the water dries up, leaving behind large areas of salt called salt pans. The salt is collected and used for cooking.

Dried salt on the surface of a salt pan.

## Adding more salt

Some of the salt in seawater is made when rocks break down and from hot-water vents on the ocean floor (see page 162). Volcanic eruptions under water also add salt to the oceans.

Clouds of steam pour from an undersea volcanic eruption.

## Albatross

The albatross can drink salt water because it has a special salt gland above its eye. The gland takes the extra salt from the bird's body and gets rid of it in a salty liquid that drips from its nostrils.

## Turtle tears

Turtles have a salt gland behind their eyes, just like the albatross. By getting rid of salt through their eyes, nostrils or tongue, turtles can live in salt water without becoming ill.

**DID YOU KNOW?**

The water in the Dead Sea in the Middle East is 10 times saltier than in the oceans. A person can float on the surface and not sink because the salty water is heavier than normal water and pushes harder against objects floating in it.

# Living in water

Animals that live in water are called aquatic animals. Their bodies are adapted to life in water. Fish have gills to breathe under water, while seals have flippers to help them swim.

## Sharks

Sharks are fish, and they breathe using gills. Water enters through their mouths and passes through the gills, where the oxygen is removed. Then the water leaves through the gill slits.

Most sharks have five gill slits on each side of their head.

## Crabs

A crab has a heavy outer skeleton covering its body. The crab's body is flat so that it can easily squeeze under and between rocks.

24

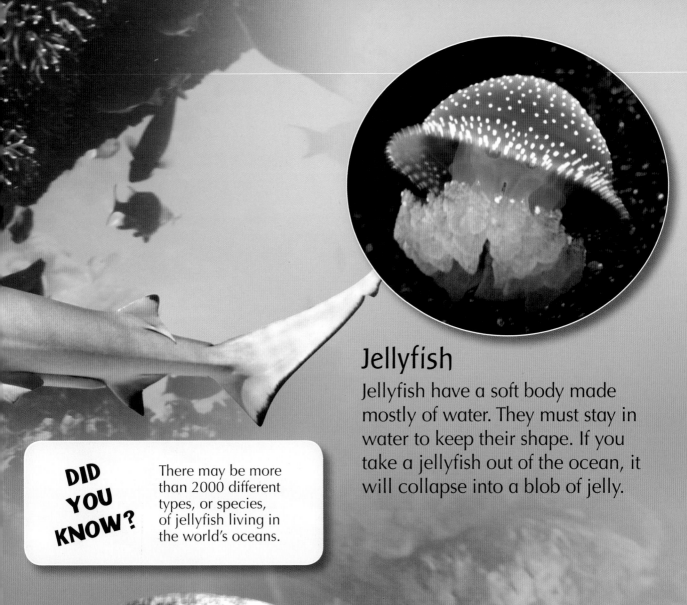

## Jellyfish

Jellyfish have a soft body made mostly of water. They must stay in water to keep their shape. If you take a jellyfish out of the ocean, it will collapse into a blob of jelly.

**DID YOU KNOW?** There may be more than 2000 different types, or species, of jellyfish living in the world's oceans.

## Seals

Seals are marine mammals with flippers instead of arms and legs. Although seals live in water, they breathe air and have to return to land to give birth.

# Food chains

A food chain shows how nutrients pass from plants to animals as one eats the other. In the ocean, plant plankton is eaten by animal plankton, or zooplankton. The zooplankton is eaten by larger animals. These animals are then eaten by even bigger animals.

## Sharks

Many sharks have a diet of seals, turtles, fish and even large seabirds. Some sharks, however, such as the whale shark and basking shark, eat plankton and small fish.

### Plant plankton

Plant plankton are at the bottom of the ocean food chains. They are called producers because they make their own food using sunlight.

### Plant-eaters

Zooplankton, or plant-eaters, such as this crab larva, eat the producers, or plant plankton. The plant-eaters are known as primary consumers.

This great white shark has leapt out of the water to catch a seal.

## Meat-eaters

Larger animals called the secondary consumers eat the primary consumers. Secondary consumers are hunters. There are many different hunters in the ocean, including fish and squid.

## Top meat-eaters

Top carnivores, or meat-eaters, such as pelicans (above), sharks and dolphins, eat fish. A top carnivore is an animal that no other animal eats – they are at the top of the ocean food chain.

# Beneath the surface

Imagine if you could walk into the sea from a beach. First you would walk through the shallow water of the continental shelf that extends out from the coast. Then the sea bed slopes down for thousands of metres to the deep ocean floor.

## Ocean levels

In some places the continental shelf is narrow, but in others it stretches for hundreds of kilometres. The continental slope links the continental shelf with the ocean floor, which may be thousands of metres down.

Sea level

Continental shelf

## Sealions

Sealions swim in the shallow water close to the shore above the continental shelf. They like to pull themselves out of the water and lie on sandy beaches.

## Starfish

Starfish are found on the continental shelf. They crawl over the sand hunting for mussels and other shellfish to eat.

DID
YOU
KNOW?

The deepest-known part of the ocean is the Mariana Trench in the Pacific Ocean. It lies 11 kilometres below sea level.

## Hammerhead

Sharks, such as this hammerhead shark, are found in both shallow and deep water. Some sharks can dive down several thousand metres to the bottom of the oceans.

Different creatures are found at each depth of the ocean.

## Spider crab

Spider crabs are creatures of the sea bed. They have been found on the ocean floor more than 3000 metres below the water's surface.

Continental slope

Ocean floor

29

# Diving

People cannot live in water, but they can dive underwater. Divers can take a deep breath and swim underwater for a minute or so, but they need a supply of air to stay for longer.

### Diving helmet

Early divers wore heavy diving helmets. Air was pumped from the surface into the helmets through rubber tubes.

## Breathing underwater

Scuba divers carry a tank of air to breathe underwater. The tank is connected to a regulator which the diver places in his or her mouth. When the diver breathes in, air flows through the regulator into the mouth.

Regulator

# Exploring reefs

Many divers like to explore coral reefs. These are good places to find brightly coloured fish and other marine creatures, such as dolphins and sea turtles.

# Discovering wrecks

Shipwrecks in shallow water are popular dive sites. By exploring a wreck, divers can learn a lot about the history of the ship. They may even discover gold coins and other valuables in the wreckage.

This submersible has a strong frame made from titanium metal up to 5 centimetres thick.

NORTH AMERICA

SOUTH AMERICA

# Exploring the deep ocean

The deep ocean is very cold and the huge pressure would crush a human instantly. Scientists use hi-tech equipment to explore this part of the ocean.

## Submersibles

Submersibles are specially designed mini submarines that can dive to depths of 4500 metres. Inside there is room for only two or three people.

## ROVs

Remotely operated vehicles (ROVs) are controlled from the surface of the water. These vehicles have mechanical arms to pick up objects, and cameras to film any strange creatures.

## Underwater features

Using technology such as submersibles, scientists have made maps of some of the ocean floor. They have found mountain ranges, such as the Mid Atlantic Ridge, and deep valleys, such as the Mariana Trench in the Pacific Ocean.

EUROPE

Atlantic Ocean

The Mid Atlantic Ridge runs down the middle of the Atlantic Ocean.

AFRICA

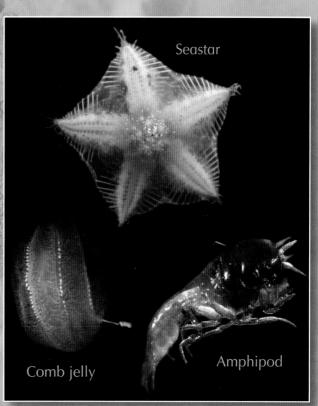

Seastar

Comb jelly

Amphipod

## Deep-sea creatures

Scientists have discovered amazing creatures living deep underwater. They include seastars, blind shrimp-like creatures called amphipods and comb jellies, which can produce their own light.

# Beaches and shores

The world's beaches and shores stretch for thousands of kilometres around every continent and island. There are rocky cliffs, sandy beaches, oozing mudflats and hot mangrove swamps. The coast is a meeting place between the sea and the land.

# Changing coasts

Coasts are never the same for very long. At high tide the shore is covered in salty seawater while at low tide the coast is exposed to the sun and wind.

## Rocky beaches

The constant battering of waves against a cliff wears away the rocks. Eventually, the cliff crumbles and rocks fall, creating a rocky beach. Over time, more and more rock ends up in the sea.

Groynes

## Protecting beaches

Groynes are special walls built on a beach to protect the coast from battering waves. The groynes slow down the waves and trap the shingle, or sand, so it is not carried away.

## Sea arches

Soft rocks along a coast wear away faster than hard rocks, creating bays. The hard rocks form headlands. These headland rocks slowly wear away, first creating caves, then arches.

This sea arch has formed on the south coast of the UK.

## Spits

A spit is a narrow strip of land that is formed when the tides remove sand from one beach and drop it further along the coast.

Sand spit

A sand spit in New Zealand.

# Rocky shores

When beaches are covered with rocks they are called rocky shores. The rocks create lots of hiding places for animals.

## Rock pools

When the tide goes out, water is trapped between the rocks. This creates rock pools, cut off from the sea until the tide returns.

## Rock shelters

Rock pools are miniature worlds. They provide shelter for plenty of animals, such as starfish (left), snails, crabs and barnacles. Some seaweeds also live in rock pools.

## Coastal creatures

Marine iguanas live in the cold Pacific Ocean around the Galápagos Islands. They are reptiles, which means that they are cold-blooded creatures. They come out of the water and sunbathe on the rocks to warm up.

## Seaweed

Seaweeds cling to the rocks surrounding the pools. Small animals, such as crabs, snails and fish hide among the seaweed.

Blenny fish _____

**DID YOU KNOW?**

The blenny, a small rock-pool fish, is also called the sea-frog because it likes to sunbathe on the rocks. It jumps back into the water with a plop if it is disturbed.

# Surviving on the rocks

Life is tough on rocky shores when the tide goes out. The animals that live on the rocks have special ways to survive out of water.

Limpets have a dome-shaped shell that can survive the battering waves.

## Limpets

Limpets feed on the tiny algae (plant life) that grow on the rocks. When the tide goes out, the limpets stick tight to the rocks so that they do not dry out.

## Mussels

Mussels attach their shells to rocks. They have two shells that are hinged together. When covered by water, mussels open their shells and feed. When the tide goes out, they shut their shells tightly together for protection.

**DID YOU KNOW?**

Limpets return to the same place every time the tide goes out. Some limpets live on the same rock all of their lives.

## Sea anemones

Most sea anemones (below) do not like being uncovered by the tide. Some survive by pulling in their tentacles – they look like a blob of jelly on the rock.

## Rock pooling

Rock pools can be explored when the tide is out. You have to be careful, however, not to get caught by the incoming tide and also not to slip on the rocks.

Tentacles

41

# Cliff life

Cliffs tower above many shorelines. They are often windy places, sprayed with salty seawater. Life is difficult for the plants and animals that make their homes high on the rocks.

## Towering cliffs

Cliffs are large lumps of rock that rise almost straight up from the shore. Most are less than 100 metres tall, but in the Hawaiian Islands there are cliffs more than 1000 metres high.

## Cliff plants

Cliff plants grow in gaps between the rocks. They grow close to the ground to stay out of the wind.

# Living on a cliff

Cliffs are home to groups, or colonies, of seabirds, such as gannets and kittiwakes. They like cliffs because predators, such as foxes and cats, cannot reach them. They lay their eggs on narrow ledges on the cliff's steep side.

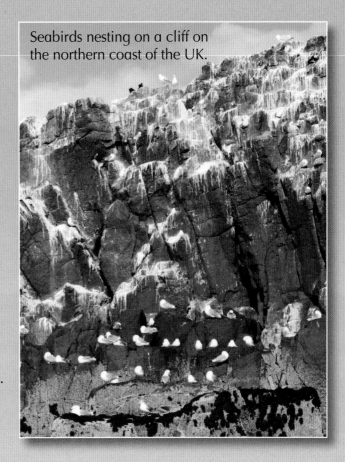

Seabirds nesting on a cliff on the northern coast of the UK.

These steep, chalk cliffs are on the coast of Dover, UK.

## Puffins

Puffins live together in large colonies on cliff tops. They make their nests in long burrows that they dig in the soil.

43

# Sandy shores

Tiny grains of sand are made as waves batter rocks into smaller and smaller pieces. Tides carry the sand along the coast and wash it up on the shore to form sandy beaches.

## Travelling coconuts

Coconut palms are a common sight on tropical beaches. When coconuts drop into the sea, they are carried by the tide to other beaches where they grow into new palms.

## Sand colonies

Soft, sandy beaches are perfect places for many sea creatures, such as seals (above), to give birth. Seals raise their young in large groups on the beaches.

# Behind the beach

Winds from the sea blow sand inland. Small piles of sand soon build up around obstacles such as fences, plants and stones. The piles of sand become gradually larger and, eventually, a sand dune is formed.

**DID YOU KNOW?**

Sand dunes are gradually blown inland by the wind. In some parts of France, sand dunes have buried whole villages.

## Sea shells

Many sea animals have shells. When these animals die their soft body rots away, leaving behind the shell. Empty shells are often washed ashore. Shells of many different shapes and sizes can be found on beaches.

# Living in sand

At first glance, little seems to live on a sandy beach, but many different animals, such as crabs and snails, are hidden in the sand. They come out of hiding when the tide comes in.

## Sand dollar

The sand dollar, above, is related to starfish and sea urchins. It has a flat body covered by spines which it uses to burrow through the sand.

## Weaver fish

Danger lurks in the sand. The weaver fish, right, has poisonous spines which stick up for protection when it has buried itself in the sand. Anybody who treads on it gets a very painful sting.

# Tidal zones

The highest point reached by the tide is called the high-tide mark, and the lowest point is the low-tide mark. The shore between these two marks is divided up into the high-, mid- and low-tide zones.

The spray zone lies above the high-tide zone.

High-tide mark

Spray zone

High-tide zone

Mid-tide zone

Low-tide zone

Low-tide mark

# Coming out to feed

Animals such as the cockle hide from predators in the sand at low tide. They emerge when the tide comes in. Cockles are hunted by many animals, including crabs, birds, fish and this colourful sun star (below).

**DID YOU KNOW?**

The razor shell gets its name from the shape of its shell, which is the shape of an old-fashioned cut-throat razor.

Cockle foot

The cockle can escape from predators by squirting a jet of water from its shell.

# Scavengers

Waves wash seaweed and other marine debris up the beach, where it collects in a line at the high-tide mark. This is called the strand line.

## Strand lines

The strand line is mostly a smelly mass of rotting seaweed, but it also contains dead bodies of fish and birds, and rubbish from passing ships.

## Scavenging crabs

Ghost crabs emerge from their sandy burrows in search of dead fish. They use their claws to tear the fish into small pieces that they can eat.

Strand lines along a beach in Thailand.

## Sandhoppers

Sandhoppers (above) are among the smallest scavengers on the strand line. These flea-like animals use their long legs to hop over the sand.

## Coastal visitors

Sometimes the dead bodies of whales and seals are washed up on to the shore. These attract animals such as brown bears and eagles. Bears that live by the coast often walk along the beach looking for food.

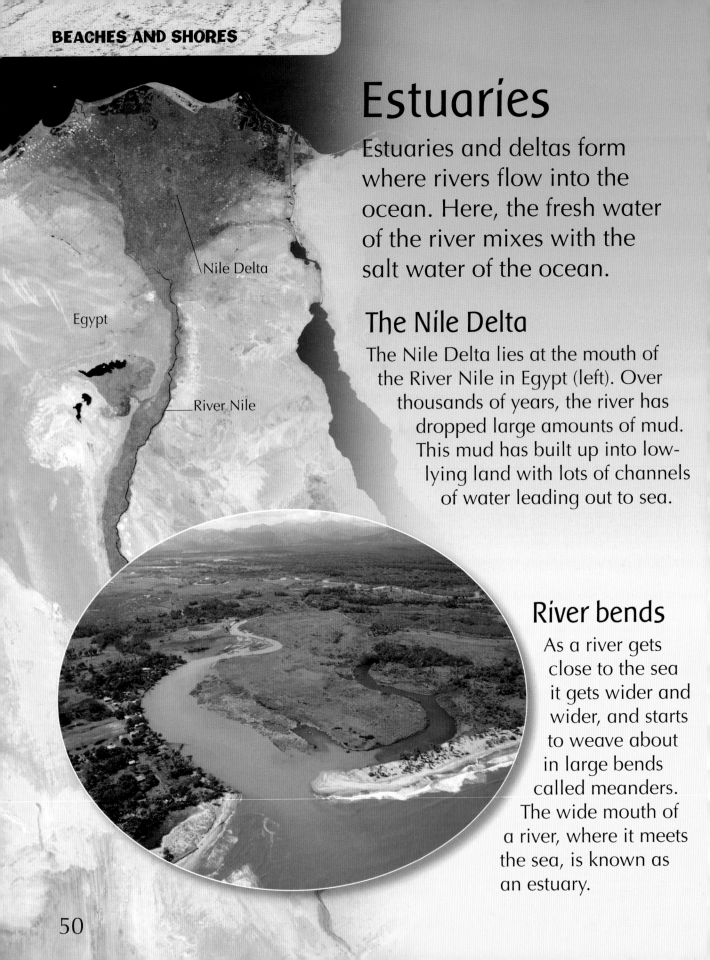

Nile Delta

Egypt

River Nile

# Estuaries

Estuaries and deltas form where rivers flow into the ocean. Here, the fresh water of the river mixes with the salt water of the ocean.

## The Nile Delta

The Nile Delta lies at the mouth of the River Nile in Egypt (left). Over thousands of years, the river has dropped large amounts of mud. This mud has built up into low-lying land with lots of channels of water leading out to sea.

## River bends

As a river gets close to the sea it gets wider and wider, and starts to weave about in large bends called meanders. The wide mouth of a river, where it meets the sea, is known as an estuary.

50

## Sea otter

Some sea otters live in the shallow water of estuaries. They hunt for crabs, mussels and snails on the sea bed. Sea otters often eat while floating on the surface of the water.

Webbed feet help sea otters swim easily through the water.

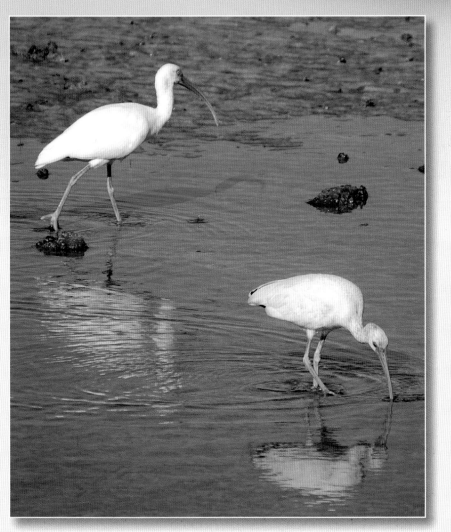

## Feeding birds

The mud at a river mouth is full of worms and snails, which attract flocks of feeding birds. Birds use their long beaks to find food in the mud.

# Mudflats

Estuary mud is thick and very smelly, but it is full of nutrients. This makes it a great home for animals such as worms and snails.

Lugworm

## Long bills

Wading birds have different-shaped bills, designed to help them feed. The oystercatcher, for example, uses its thick, straight bill to open the shells of mussels and razor shells.

## Lugworm

The lugworm digs a burrow in the mud. It sucks water into its burrow and filters out any food. Wading birds prey upon lugworms, pulling them out of their burrows.

Oystercatcher

## Snails

Mud is full of all kinds of snails, such as cockles, winkles and spire shells. Spire shells are found on the surface, but cockles lie under the mud.

This snail has a spiral shell that protects its soft body.

Both eyes are on one side of the head.

Flounder

## Flat fish

The bodies of flatfish such as a plaice, turbot or flounder are squashed from side to side. This shape is perfect for living on the sea bed. If you look closely, you will see that one eye has moved so that both are on the top.

53

# Marsh and swamp

Swamps and salt marshes lie close to the shoreline. When the tides are high enough, seawater often covers them, bringing in lots of nutrients.

Young shrimp

## Salt marshes

Salt marshes are formed when mud builds up behind banks of small stones, called shingle. Salt-loving plants, such as cord grass and sea lavender, start to grow. The marsh is criss-crossed with small streams, or creeks, that fill with salt water during high tides.

## Nurseries

Salt marshes are breeding grounds for shrimps and fish. The young shrimps and fish spend the first part of their life in the safety of the creeks before they swim out to sea.

## Marsh plants

Salt-marsh plants have to be able to live in salty ground as they are often covered by sea water. They have small, fleshy leaves that can store fresh water. Samphire (right) is a plant that grows on salt marshes and can be eaten by people.

## Alligators

Alligators are reptiles. The American alligator is found in salt marshes and swamps, where it hunts mostly fish and crabs. Larger alligators attack deer, and even eat other smaller alligators.

**DID YOU KNOW?**

More than one million alligators live in the Florida Everglades.

Alligators have powerful jaws, with many teeth, that can crush bones.

Long, broad snout.

# Mangrove swamps

Mangrove swamps are found along tropical coasts near the equator. Here, there are strange-looking trees, fish that can walk and crabs that wave to each other.

## Swamp roots

Mangrove trees look as if they are growing on stilts as their roots, supporting them in the mud, come out of the water. The tangle of roots is a great hiding place for young fish.

## Mudskippers

A mudskipper has gills, but it mostly breathes through its skin. This allows the fish to leave the water. It uses its stiff front fins to push its body across the mud and even up mangrove roots.

The tree roots come out of the mud.

## Birds of prey

Ospreys are the top hunters in a mangrove swamp. They feed on fish and small animals. They build nests, out of twigs, which they use for many years.

## Fiddler crabs

The male fiddler crab has an extra-large claw that he waves up and down as a signal to other crabs. At low tide, the male fiddler crab sits at the entrance to his burrow and waves his claw to attract females.

# Nesting on the beach

Many creatures, such as crabs and turtles, crawl on to beaches to lay their eggs. Their young hatch a few weeks later and hurry away to begin life in the ocean.

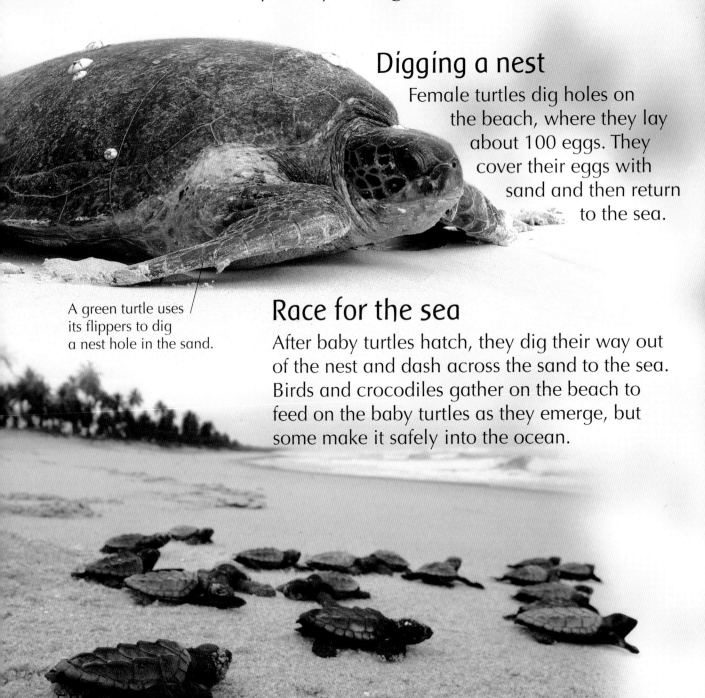

## Digging a nest

Female turtles dig holes on the beach, where they lay about 100 eggs. They cover their eggs with sand and then return to the sea.

A green turtle uses its flippers to dig a nest hole in the sand.

## Race for the sea

After baby turtles hatch, they dig their way out of the nest and dash across the sand to the sea. Birds and crocodiles gather on the beach to feed on the baby turtles as they emerge, but some make it safely into the ocean.

# Horseshoe crabs

Each spring, when there is an especially high tide, up to one million horseshoe crabs appear on the beaches of Delaware Bay, USA. Each female crab digs a small pit and lays about 20,000 eggs.

A thick, spiny shell protects the horseshoe crab from hunters.

## DID YOU KNOW?

The horseshoe crab is not really a crab. It is a distant relative of the spider. It is a very old creature, whose looks have not changed much in 300 million years.

The body of a red crab is about 13 centimetres across.

# Crab invasion

Red crabs live in the forests on Christmas Island in the Pacific Ocean. Once a year, the crabs leave the forests and walk to the ocean where they breed on the beaches. In places, millions of crabs are on the move, covering the ground.

59

# Coastal life

The shallow waters around land are full of life. Here, tiny plants called phytoplankton and animals called zooplankton float in the water. These plankton are food for large numbers of fish, which attract larger predators, such as sharks, whales and seabirds.

# Tiny plants

The moving ocean stirs up mud on the seabed. This releases nutrients into the water. These nutrients provide food for tiny plants called phytoplankton that float in the water.

Diatoms

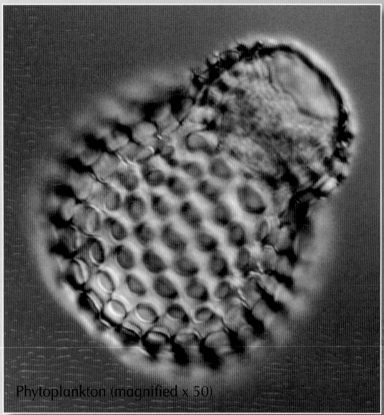

Phytoplankton (magnified x 50)

## Diatoms

Diatoms are a type of phytoplankton that have hard, shell-like skeletons. The skeleton is in two parts, called valves, that fit together tightly. There are many types of diatom, each with its own design of skeleton.

## Phytoplankton

The phytoplankton form the bottom of the marine food chain. Just like plants on land, phytoplankton can make their own food using sunlight, carbon dioxide (a gas) and nutrients from the water.

Diatoms

## Dinoflagellates

Dinoflagellates make up much of the phytoplankton. At night, these tiny organisms give out a strange light. This is called bioluminescence.

## Plankton bloom

Sometimes, there are extra nutrients in the water and the phytoplankton increase in number. There are so many plankton that the water changes colour. This is called a plankton bloom, and it can grow so large it can even be seen from space.

This large plankton bloom is off the coast of Argentina.

# Tiny animals

Phytoplankton are eaten by the creatures that make up the animal plankton, or zooplankton. These animals drift in the water, carried around by tides and currents.

## Baby fish

Many fish lay their eggs in coastal waters. When they hatch, the baby fish feed on phytoplankton. They grow quickly until they are large enough to swim out to sea.

## Microscopic creatures

Most animal plankton is made up of tiny organisms, like copepods and amphipods (above). The larvae of marine animals such as starfish, jellyfish and barnacles are also called animal plankton.

## Jellyfish

Jellyfish are among the largest animal plankton. They have a bell-shaped body and long tentacles, which hang below. Many just drift in the water, while others swim by flapping their bell-shaped body.

## Salps

Salps are tube-like organisms about the size of a large peanut. They suck in water and food. Where there is plenty of food there are large swarms of salps.

Salps may link together to form chains that are up to 5 metres long.

## Filter feeders

Most plankton feeders filter, or sieve, tiny organisms from the water. Humpback whales (left) have frilly plates called baleen in their mouth that sieve the water. Others, such as the basking shark, sieve food from the water through their gills.

# Plankton feeders

Animal and plant plankton are the favourite food of many animals including ocean giants such as the blue whale, whale shark and basking shark.

## Big mouth

The basking shark swims along with its mouth wide open. When its mouth is full of water, the fish closes it and squeezes the water out through its gill slits. Any food is trapped inside by rakers (bristle-like filters) in the gills.

# Manta ray

Most rays live on the seabed, hunting fish and small animals. The huge manta ray (left) is different. It is an active fish that swims great distances, filtering plankton through its gills.

## Ocean wanderer

A whale shark's spots are unique, and can be used to recognise each shark.

The whale shark is the largest fish in the world. It grows up to 13 metres long and can weigh more than 20 tonnes. It is a filter feeder and, despite its size, it is not a dangerous shark.

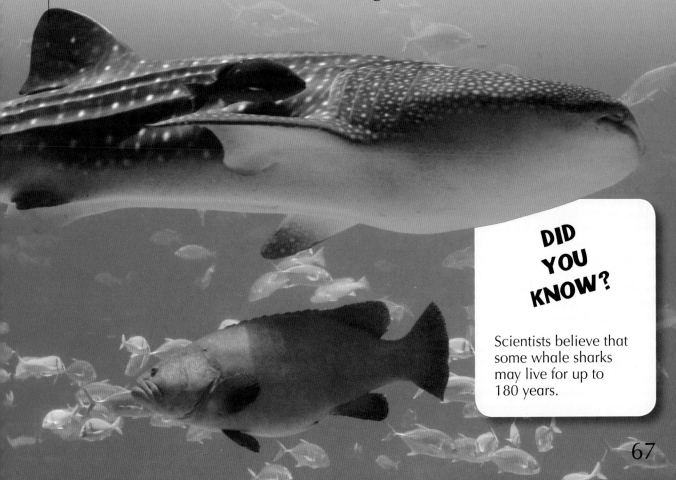

**DID YOU KNOW?**

Scientists believe that some whale sharks may live for up to 180 years.

# Krill

Krill are among the most important animals in the ocean. There are billions of these small, shrimp-like animals. They are eaten by whales, seals, penguins and seabirds.

Krill

## Living in numbers

Krill live in large groups, called swarms. Up to 30,000 krill can be found in a cubic metre of water (enough to fill four baths). The wriggling swarm confuses hunters.

## Penguin predator

Krill are an important food for penguins. Chinstrap penguins (right) feed on larger types of krill, while Adélie penguins prefer the smaller ones. Penguins, together with whales, seals and other seabirds, eat about 150–300 million tonnes of krill each year.

## Raised on krill

Young leopard seals feed almost entirely on krill. As they get older, they eat bigger fish. The adults are dangerous predators that hunt penguins and other seals.

The leopard seal sieves krill from the water through its large, jagged teeth.

## Squid

Squid swim through the water by pushing a jet of water out of their body. They catch krill using their long tentacles. Their sharp beaks rip the krill into small pieces for swallowing.

Squid

Holdfast

# Seaweed

Seaweeds are found in shallow water close to the coast. They are not proper plants as they do not have leaves, stems or roots, but they do make their own food.

## Holding on

Seaweeds have sticky knobs called holdfasts. These grip to the rocks to prevent the seaweed from being washed away by the tides.

## Covering rocks

Many seaweeds are found on rocky shores. When they are covered by the tide, their leaf-like fronds float in the water. When the tide goes out, they are left piled up on the rocks until the tide returns.

Oarweed (brown seaweed)     Dead man's fingers (green seaweed)     Bladder wrack (brown seaweed)

## Types of seaweed

There are three main types of seaweed – green, brown and red. Brown seaweed is the most common and is found on rocky beaches. Green seaweed is found only in very shallow water.

### DID YOU KNOW?

Seaweeds range in size from just a few centimetres to more than 60 metres long.

### Harvesting seaweed

People harvest seaweed from the sea. It is eaten as a vegetable in Japan and other countries. Seaweeds are also used as an ingredient in skin cream, shampoo, nail polish, ice cream, beer and paint, and as a fertilizer on soil.

# Kelp forests

Kelp are large, brown seaweeds that grow closely together. Kelp forests, with their fronds gently moving in the water, are magical places where many animals live.

## Thin leaves

Kelp have a stalk with long, thin leaves, called fronds, at the top. They are covered in a protective layer of mucus and feel quite tough, but are easily damaged in storms.

**DID YOU KNOW?**

There are different types of kelp. The giant kelp is the fastest growing of all. It can increase the length of its fronds by up to 60 centimetres every day.

## Dense growth

Kelp forests are found in fairly shallow water, where they can get enough sunlight to make their food. At the surface, they form a thick, tangled mat.

## Floating plant

A kelp has a balloon-like float at the base of the fronds. The float is full of air. It keeps the fronds floating near the water's surface, where there is more sunlight.

A diver explores kelp forests off the coast of California, USA.

## Kelp eater

Sea urchins eat kelp. In some places, there are too many sea urchins. They eat the young kelp before it has a chance to grow – so the forest disappears.

# Kelp forest animals

More than 800 types of animal have been found living in kelp forests. There are shoals of brightly coloured fish, feeding limpets, lurking blue sharks and giant rays.

## Forest hunter

The blue shark is a regular visitor to the kelp forest. It hides in the kelp waiting for prey, such as squid, to pass close by.

Blue shark

## Eagle ray

The eagle ray (below) has huge wing-like fins that are up to 2 metres wide. It turns on its side to swim between the stalks of the kelp.

## Sea otter

Sea otters (right) feed on sea urchins and clams that they find in the kelp forests. Clams have hard shells so otters collect stones, which they use to crack open the shells. They balance the stone on their stomach as they hit the clam shell against it.

## Garibaldi fish

The bright orange garibaldi fish aggressively defends its nest site in the kelp from all – including divers! The male builds a nest in which the female lays her eggs. He then looks after the eggs until they hatch.

### DID YOU KNOW?

Sea otters sometimes wrap themselves in kelp. They use it as an anchor so that they do not drift away while they sleep.

# Sea grass

There are underwater sea grass meadows along sheltered coasts. The sea grass shelters large numbers of fish and attracts animals such as manatees and dolphins.

## Underwater grass

Sea grass gets its name from its grass-like appearance, but it is not a proper grass. It is a plant that can grow, rooted in sand, in shallow sea water.

## Manatee

The manatee, or sea cow, looks a bit like a hippopotamus. It has paddle-like front legs to push itself through the water. It uses its large upper lip to graze the sea grass. An adult eats up to 50 kilogrammes of grass every day.

# Sea horse

The sea horse swims upright in the water using three small fins. It wraps its long tail around the sea grass so that it is not carried away on the currents.

A sea horse's long snout acts like a vacuum cleaner, sucking up tiny shrimps.

**DID YOU KNOW?**

Female sea horses lay their eggs inside a pouch in the male's belly. Four weeks later, he gives birth to up to 1000 baby sea horses.

## Lobster nursery

Sea grass meadows are nurseries for spiny lobsters. Adult lobsters come here to lay their eggs, which hatch into baby lobsters. When the lobsters are big enough, they move to nearby swamps and coral reefs.

# Seabirds

The rich harvest of fish in coastal waters attracts a wide variety of seabirds, including pelicans, gulls, gannets and cormorants. Seabirds can often be seen swooping down to the water in search of fish to eat.

## Gannets

Gannets live in colonies on sea cliffs. They dive into the sea from a height of about 30 metres, and catch fish under the water using their pointed bills.

## Pelicans

White pelicans often fish in groups. Together, they chase fish into shallow water where they are easier to catch. The pelicans scoop up the fish in the pouch under their bill, and then toss them down their throat.

### DID YOU KNOW?

There are about 50,000 pairs of gannets nesting on Bass Rock, off the east coast of Scotland.

Gannets have long, narrow wings. The wings measure almost 2 metres from tip to tip.

## Cormorants

A cormorant (left) can dive to depths of over 40 metres. It then swims underwater using its large, webbed feet. Its hooked bill is perfect for gripping slippery fish.

## Following whales

Seabirds such as gulls (right) gather around whales as they feed near the surface of the ocean. Whales drive lots of fish and krill to the surface of the water, where the birds can reach them.

# Baleen whales

Baleen whales are huge mammals that have comb-like plates hanging from the roof of their mouth. They use these baleen plates to sieve plankton and small fish from the water.

Whale's baleen plate

## Baleen plates

A whale's baleen plates are made from keratin – like your fingernails are. The teeth of these plates are known as whalebones.

## Blowholes

A blowhole is a whale's nostril, found on top of its head. Whales cannot breathe underwater, so they have to take a deep breath before they dive. When they return to the surface air is forced from their lungs through the blowhole, which sprays water into the air.

Blue whale

# Blue whale

At over 30 metres long, the blue whale (right) is the world's largest animal. It eats up to 7 tonnes of krill a day. During the day, it feeds at depths of 100 metres. But at night it follows the krill, which move to the surface to feed.

Grooves in this humpback whale's throat allow the throat to expand to four times its usual size when it is feeding.

# Breaching

Whales sometimes leap out of the water and fall down with a big splash. This is called breaching. Scientists are unsure why they do this. It may be to signal to other whales, or it may be to remove parasites from their skin.

# Toothed whales

Orcas, pilot whales, dolphins and porpoises are toothed whales. Toothed whales usually live together in small groups called pods. They are hunters that feed mostly on fish and squid.

## Arctic whales

The beluga whale (left) and the narwhal live in the freezing waters of the Arctic Ocean. The beluga has white skin, which is good camouflage against the ice.

## Sharp teeth

Most toothed whales have small, cone-shaped teeth, which are perfect for gripping slippery fish. Orcas (killer whales) have about 50 teeth, but dolphins can have up to 100 teeth.

The dorsal fin on the back of a dolphin has a wave-like shape.

A pair of dolphins

# Dolphin or porpoise?

Dolphins and porpoises look very similar, but a dolphin has a pointed snout and a long, slim body. A porpoise has a rounded fish-like snout and a shorter, rounder body.

## Hunting seals

Some orcas living off the coast of South America have learnt how to surf on to beaches to catch seals. The whales have to be careful not to become stranded on the beach.

# Coastal nurseries

Many animals visit coastal waters to breed or to have their young. These shallow waters are often sheltered, and there is plenty of food for the young animals.

Hammerhead sharks gathering to breed.

## Hammerhead gathering

Each year, hammerhead sharks gather together in special breeding places. Each male selects a female, and they then mate. After about 10 months, the female swims into shallow water to give birth to her pups.

## Laying eggs

Many squid live in shallow water close to rocks, caves and sea grass. The female lays eggs with a short stalk, which she attaches to rocks and seaweeds so that they do not get carried away by the tides.

Squid eggs

## Underwater flier

Manta rays live in the deep sea but give birth in shallow coastal waters, where the young stay for several years. The females are pregnant for about a year before giving birth to one or two pups.

Manta ray

## Whale migration

Many whales make regular journeys along the world's coasts. Humpback whales spend the summer in cold waters, where there is plenty of food. They then travel, or migrate, to warmer, shallow water, where the females give birth.

## DID YOU KNOW?

The yearly migration of grey whales from Baja California, to the Arctic and back is a distance of about 20,000 kilometres – the longest journey made by any mammal.

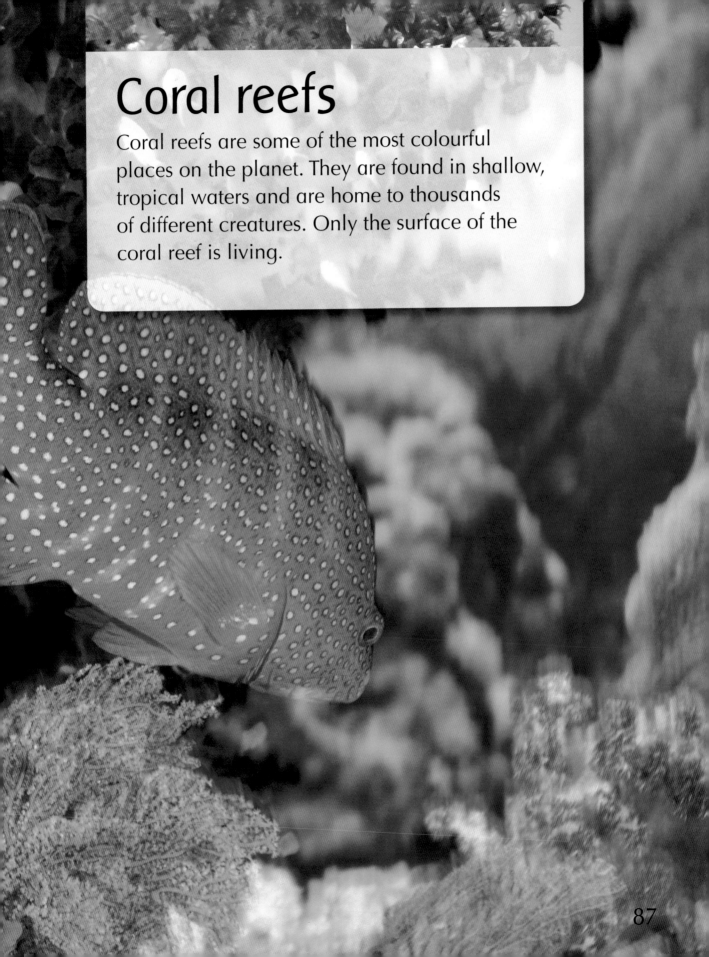

# Coral reefs

Coral reefs are some of the most colourful places on the planet. They are found in shallow, tropical waters and are home to thousands of different creatures. Only the surface of the coral reef is living.

# Where in the world?

Coral reefs are found in warm seas, where the water is shallow and there is plenty of light. Coral will grow only in clean water that is free from pollution.

## Reefs around the world

Most coral reefs are found in the Indian and Pacific Oceans, the Caribbean and the Red Sea. Corals are not found where there are cold ocean currents or where large rivers flow into the sea.

Greenland

Arctic Ocean

NORTH AMERICA

EUROPE

ASIA

Atlantic Ocean

AFRICA

Pacific Ocean

Pacific Ocean

SOUTH AMERICA

Indian Ocean

AUSTRALIA

Coral reefs

Southern Ocean

## Bathed in sunlight

Corals need sunlight because they have tiny algae, called zooxanthellae, in their cells. These algae use the sunlight to make their own food. The algae also provide the corals with food. In return, they get shelter and protection.

## Exposed coral

Some coral reefs close to the shore are exposed when the tide goes out. The exposed coral is then damaged by the sun and wind.

## Great Barrier Reef

The Great Barrier Reef is the world's largest coral reef. It runs along the northeast coast of Australia and is 2500 kilometres long. Almost 6000 different species of animal live on this reef.

**DID YOU KNOW?**

The Great Barrier Reef is the largest structure made by living creatures on Earth. It is so large that it can even be seen from space.

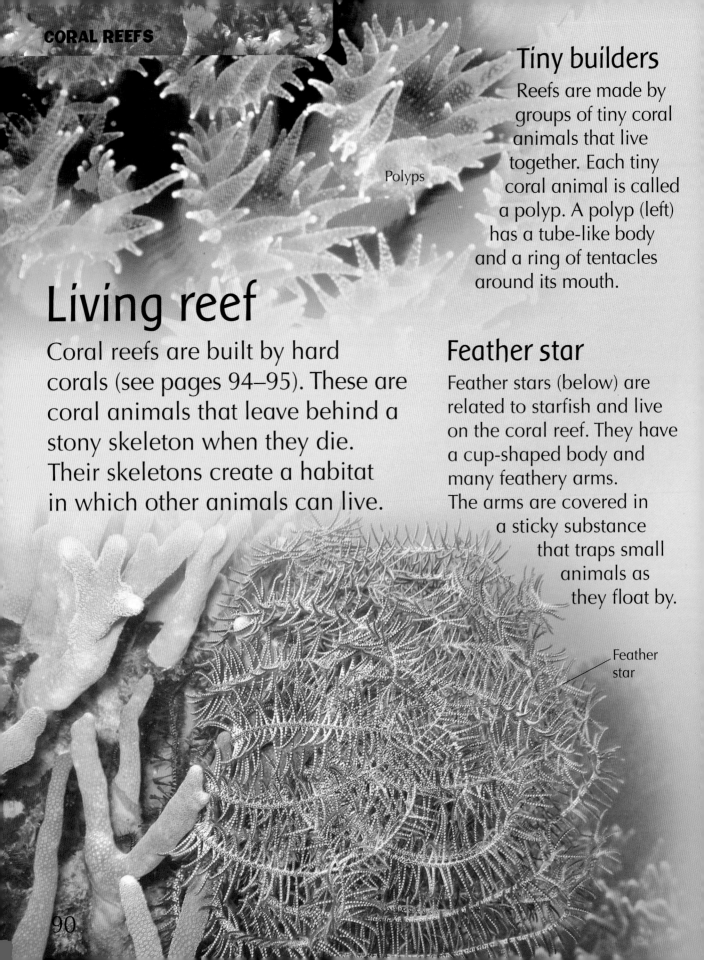

## Tiny builders

Reefs are made by groups of tiny coral animals that live together. Each tiny coral animal is called a polyp. A polyp (left) has a tube-like body and a ring of tentacles around its mouth.

Polyps

# Living reef

Coral reefs are built by hard corals (see pages 94–95). These are coral animals that leave behind a stony skeleton when they die. Their skeletons create a habitat in which other animals can live.

## Feather star

Feather stars (below) are related to starfish and live on the coral reef. They have a cup-shaped body and many feathery arms. The arms are covered in a sticky substance that traps small animals as they float by.

Feather star

## Living in crevices

Many animals, such as the moray eel (right), hide in the cracks and crevices on the reef. The moray eel darts out and grabs any small fish that swim too close.

## Sponges

Sponges are animals, but they do not move around. Some sponges grow to about 2 metres tall. Others form a flat, crust-like growth over the surface of the reef.

Vase sponges

**DID YOU KNOW?**

There are more than 5000 different types of sponge. Some of the largest may be many hundreds of years old.

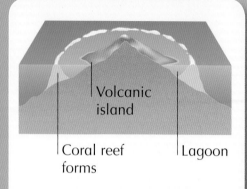

Volcanic
island

Coral reef
forms

Lagoon

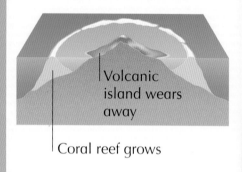

Volcanic
island wears
away

Coral reef grows

Coral atoll

## How an atoll forms

Atolls take millions of years
to form. Volcanoes create
islands in the oceans. Then
coral animals build reefs
around the islands. Over a
long time, the volcanic
islands wear away but the
reefs keep growing – leaving
behind the atoll rings.

# Types of reef

There are three types of reef.
A fringing reef is formed by corals
that follow a coastline, while a
barrier reef grows further away from
the land. An atoll is a circular reef
around an area of shallow water,
called a lagoon.

## Coral atolls

A coral atoll (above) is a ring of coral
reef surrounding a lagoon. The coral reef
protects the lagoon from the ocean waves.
Most of the world's atolls are found in
the Indian and Pacific Oceans.

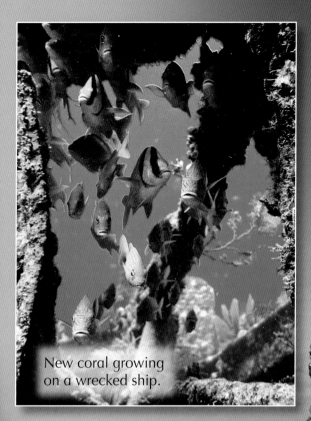
New coral growing
on a wrecked ship.

## New coral

Coral polyps like to
grow on something
hard. They will even
make their home
on the remains of
a sunken ship.

## Coral sand

Waves batter against the
coral reef, and the reef
gradually wears away.
The tiny particles of reef
are washed up on the
shore as sand, eventually
creating beautiful
tropical beaches.

A beach with
fine coral sand

# Hard corals

Hard corals are those with limestone skeletons. There are many different species of hard coral, each forming an interesting shape on the reef.

## Table coral

Table coral (below) is a fast-growing, spreading coral that forms a flat, table-like shape. It grows to several metres across and is made up of lots of short branches.

## Brain coral

Brain coral (above) gets its name from the way it looks like the folded surface of a real brain. These corals grow up to 1.8 metres tall, and are strong enough to survive in rough seas.

# Mushroom coral

The mushroom coral (right) is round or oval in shape. It can be flat or domed and is usually about 50 centimetres across. Most corals are made up of many polyps, but this type has just one large one.

# Black coral

Black corals (right) are found in deeper water, where there is less light. They are branching corals, which look a bit like bushes with little branches. The skeleton is black but the polyps are white, yellow or orange.

# Soft coral

Soft corals come in a wide range of colours such as red, yellow, orange and purple. Soft corals are those that do not have a hard skeleton.

## Feeding corals

Coral polyps feed by extending their tentacles into the water to catch small animals. The tentacles are covered in stinging cells, which they use to kill their prey and to defend themselves.

## Underwater fans

Fan corals (above) form beautiful fan shapes, up to 3 metres across, which move gently in the currents. Each fan has a flexible stem fixing it firmly to the rocks.

**DID YOU KNOW?**

Soft coral is known as a flower animal because it can take on many different shapes and colours.

Yellow finger gorgonian coral

# Whip coral

Whip corals (below) look a bit like long drinking straws. They bend in the ocean currents, catching plankton to eat, but do not get damaged.

## Fire coral

Fire corals have a powerful sting. This protects the polyps from coral-eating fish. Fire corals are often found on the edge of the reef as they can survive in rough water.

Clown fish

# Living together

Animals live closely together on the reef. Some depend on others for a home, to stay clean or for protection from predators.

## Living with stings

Anemones are covered in sting cells. Most animals stay away, but not the clown fish. It lives in the safety of the tentacles as it is covered with a slimy mucus that protects it from the stings.

## Living camouflage

The hermit crab protects its soft body by living inside an empty shell. Anemones have attached themselves to this hermit crab's shell (left). The anemones provide the crab with camouflage and protection and, in return, the crab helps the anemones to find food.

# Cleaning station

Fish have difficulty removing the tiny parasites that live on their body, so they visit 'cleaning stations'. Here, small fish and cleaner shrimps remove and eat the parasites for them.

# Wash and brush-up

The moray eel (below) opens its mouth so that the cleaner shrimps can remove parasites from every nook and cranny.

Kissing surgeon          Wrasse

## DID YOU KNOW?

Decorator crabs attach sponges and seaweeds to their shell. These living decorations help to disguise the crab from predators.

# Eating coral

Coral is an important source of food for many reef animals, including turtles, starfish, snails and lots of fish.

## Fish with beaks

The parrot fish uses its large, beak-like teeth to bite off lumps of coral covered in algae, crunching them into small pieces. Much of the coral passes through its gut and ends up as sand on a beach!

## Hawksbill turtle

This turtle (right) has a pointed beak. It is perfect for reaching into crevices on the reef to find sponges – its favourite food.

The parrot fish gets its name from the teeth at the front of its mouth, which look like a parrot's beak.

## Butterfly fish

Butterfly fish (above) have a flat body and a long, thin snout. They are the perfect shape to pick up small animals from inside coral crevices. Butterfly fish have colourful patterns – just like butterflies!

## Reef devourer

The large crown-of-thorns starfish (right) has a huge appetite for coral. It has up to 18 arms and is covered with poisonous spines. At night, it crawls on to coral and empties its stomach contents. The digestive juices turn the coral into a liquid, which the starfish then sucks up.

# Hunters on the reef

The thousands of fish and small animals living on the reef attract a lot of predators. These include barracuda, octopuses and lion fish.

## Barracuda

The barracuda (above) has powerful jaws, knife-like teeth and a long body. It hangs in the water without moving, then darts forward to grab prey with a burst of speed.

## Lizard fish

The lizard fish sits on the reef propped up on its front fins with its head raised. It darts forward to catch prey, such as small fish.

## Lion fish

This is a
dangerous fish
– its spines are
tipped with poison.
Lion fish trap prey using
their large, spiny fins – and
then swallow it whole.

## Reef octopus

The reef octopus hides in holes with
just its legs sticking out. It grabs its
prey of fish or clams with its suckers
and pulls it towards its mouth.
The octopus then uses its powerful
beak to crush its meal.

**DID
YOU
KNOW?**
Young barracudas
live in large shoals
consisting of several
thousand fish.

103

# Reef sharks

Sharks are among the most feared animals on the reef. Large reef sharks cruise along the reef edge looking for fish, while smaller sharks hunt shrimps and crabs amongst the corals.

Blacktip reef shark

## Underwater zebra

Adult zebra sharks (right) have spots, but when they are young they have stripes, just like a zebra. Their downward-pointing mouth is designed to pick up clams from the sea bed. They also hunt crabs and small fish.

## White-tipped reef shark

The white-tipped reef shark is browny grey in colour, but has white tips on its fins. It rests during the day, and hunts for food at night in the crevices of the coral reef.

A white-tipped reef shark resting under a coral ledge.

**DID YOU KNOW?**

There have only ever been two recorded attacks on scuba divers by blacktip reef sharks.

## Blacktip reef shark

Blacktip sharks are the top predators on the reef as they are not hunted by any other animals. This shark hunts in shallow water and lagoons. It catches sea snakes as well as fish and octopuses.

## Laying eggs

Some types of shark lay eggs. Each egg is protected inside a tough leathery case. Curly threads attach the case to seaweed so that it is not swept away. The egg case of the dogfish shark (right) is called a mermaid's purse.

# Reef defence

Reef animals protect themselves from predators in different ways. Some use body armour or poisons to defend themselves. Others rely on camouflage to keep them hidden on the reef.

## Body armour

Seahorses use body armour to defend themselves. The tough armour gives them good protection, but makes swimming more difficult. They stay still much of the time, relying on their camouflage to hide them from hungry hunters.

## Hiding in coral

Corals make great hiding places for the creatures that live on them. Tiny animals, such as this small goby (left), hide from their predators on and among the coral branches.

**DID YOU KNOW?**

The reef stonefish is one of the most poisonous fish in the world. It has 13 spines, which inject poison into anything that touches them.

## Frog camouflage

Frog fish (above) look more like a piece of coral or sponge than a fish. By keeping perfectly still, they blend in with the reef and are difficult for predators to spot.

## Spiny defence

The cowfish's spiky body armour, with long spines over each eye, gives it an unusual appearance. If the cowfish is attacked, it can also release a poison into the water from its skin.

# Out at night

The reef is active at night as many of the animals are nocturnal. They hide during the day in caves and crevices, then come out to feed in the safety of the dark.

## Cardinal fish

The female cardinal fish lays her eggs in the water, where they are fertilized by the male. The male then collects them in his mouth and cares for them until they hatch. He releases the young fish in the safety of darkness.

Cardinal fish

## Night-time crab

The arrow crab is a night-time scavenger. It clambers over coral looking for the remains of animals that have died on the reef.

The arrow crab has eight spider-like legs and two legs that end in claws.

108

## Safety in numbers

Snappers (above) are seen at night swimming around in small groups. They hunt crabs, shrimps, worms and fish that live on sandy sea beds near reefs.

## Squirrel fish

Squirrel fish have extra-large eyes. The fish hide in caves and wrecked ships by day, and come out at night to feed on plankton.

**DID YOU KNOW?**

Cardinal fish carry their eggs around in their mouth for 18 to 24 days before they hatch.

# Reef molluscs

Molluscs are a group of animals that include snails, clams and squid. Most molluscs have a muscular 'foot', which they use to move around.

## Shell protection

A heavy shell, such as this helmet shell, protects the soft body of a snail. When threatened, the snail retreats into its shell. This is a spiral shell, but some are cone-shaped.

## Giant clam

The giant clam is a bivalve – a snail with two shells that are hinged together. Clams stay in one place on the reef, sucking water into their body and filtering out plankton. Their colour comes from algae, which live in their cells and provide the clams with food.

# Nudibranch

Nudibranches are soft-bodied sea slugs that have no shell. Without a shell for protection, they use poison to defend themselves against predators. They are brightly coloured to warn other animals that they are poisonous.

## Coral eaters

These flamingo tongue snails (right) are coral eaters. As they crawl over the coral, their feet release digestive juices. The juices dissolve the polyps, and the snails absorb the nutrients through their foot.

**DID YOU KNOW?**

The largest giant clams grow to more than a metre across, weigh more than 200 kilogrammes and can live for up to 100 years.

The shell of a tongue snail is white. The spots are on a thin layer that covers the shell.

# Open oceans

Stretching beyond the coastal water is the vast, open ocean. It covers thousands of kilometres and extends down for thousands of metres. The open ocean may look empty at first glance, but there are many different kinds of animal living beneath the surface. These range from tiny microscopic creatures to whales – the largest animals that have ever lived on the planet.

# Surface waters

The open oceans are home to fewer animals than coral reefs and coastal waters. Most animals that do live here are found in the surface layer, which is the top 200 metres.

## Light in the water

The ocean's surface is lit by sunlight. The top 30 metres is brightly lit, but it gets darker as you go deeper. By 200 metres, all sunlight has gone and the water looks bluey-black.

## Flying fish

The flying fish has an unusual way of escaping predators. When threatened, it swims straight at the surface of the water and flies into the air, using its fins like wings. It can glide above the surface for up to 100 metres.

# Surface waves

When the wind blows over the surface of the ocean it creates waves. As the waves grow larger they are moved along by the wind, and this helps to mix up the water.

The wind blowing over the surface of the sea pushes along wind-powered boats, such as this yacht.

## Humpback whales

Whales, such as these humpback whales, have to come to the surface to breathe. Most whales swim near the surface of the ocean, and dive deeper only to find food.

## DID YOU KNOW?

During storms at sea, it is not unusual for waves to reach more than 30 metres in height. That is as tall as a 10-storey building!

115

# Floating life

The surface layer is home to many floating animals, both large and small. These are carried across the ocean by the currents and waves.

## Floating stings

The Portuguese man-of-war (left) looks like a jellyfish (see pages 118–19), but it is a colony of individual polyps called a siphonophore. One polyp floats above the surface to catch the wind. Others form hanging tentacles to trap food.

## Comb jellies

Comb jellies look like jellyfish without any tentacles. The body is just a few centimetres long. When comb jellies catch the light, they shimmer in rainbow colours.

## Siphonophores

Like all siphonophores, this deep-water species (right) is formed from a colony of individuals – each with a different job to do. Its long, stinging tentacles dangle in the water to catch fish and shrimp.

## Tiny squid

The larvae of squid and fish are found in the surface layer, where they drift in the currents. These tiny larvae hunt even smaller animals, such as copepods and amphipods.

These squid larvae use their short tentacles to catch small animals.

**DID YOU KNOW?**

The world's longest animal is a species of siphonophore. It can grow to more than 40 metres in length.

# Jellyfish

Jellyfish are not actually fish. They are invertebrates with a jelly-like body, and are related to corals and sea anemones.

## Floating bells

Jellyfish have a soft, bell-shaped body with tentacles hanging beneath the bell. Each tentacle is covered in cells that can sting or kill other creatures.

This jellyfish has tentacles covered in stinging cells.

## Underwater moons

Most jellyfish float in the water and are carried around by currents. Some can swim very slowly by squeezing water in and out of their bell – which looks a bit an umbrella opening and closing.

# Lion's mane

The largest jellyfish is the lion's mane. Its bell is more than a metre across and the tentacles are many metres long. They eat almost anything that bumps into their tentacles.

# Sea nettles

Sea nettles (below) are a small type of jellyfish. Each year, in some parts of the world, swarms of sea nettles gather together to lay eggs. Sea nettles can sting, so people and marine animals stay away from these areas.

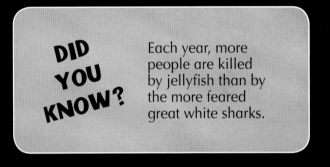

**DID YOU KNOW?** Each year, more people are killed by jellyfish than by the more feared great white sharks.

# Shoals of fish

Many fish live together in groups called shoals. Some shoals contain just a few fish but, when shoals join together, a huge shoal of hundreds of thousands of fish may form.

## Living in groups

Fish are safer in large groups. A shoal of fish confuses hunters by darting around in different directions. The fish use their senses to make sure that they do not bump into each other.

A shoal of mullet leap out of the water to escape a dolphin.

A shoal of fish move away from an approaching diver.

## Jumping to escape

When a group of dolphins finds a shoal they surround it and then chase the fish. Some fish leap out of the water to try to escape.

## Bigeye jacks

These fish are powerful hunters with large eyes and a forked tail. They patrol the oceans in large shoals seeking out smaller fish, which they catch in their large jaws.

## Huge shoals

Sardines (right) form huge shoals. These attract hunters such as dolphins, sharks and swordfish. Sardines are an important link in ocean food chains (see pages 30–31).

# Catching fish

Fish are an important part of our diet. Each year, large fishing boats called trawlers catch millions of tonnes of fish.

## Trawling the seas

People living along the coast have always fished the seas. Over time, the size of the fishing boats and their nets have increased. Modern trawlers stay at sea for longer and use the latest equipment to find fish.

## Various fish

Thousands of different types of fish are regularly caught around the world. Only about 20 types are fished in large quantities. These fish fall into five groups – cod, herring, jacks, mackerel and redfish.

This beam trawler has two nets. Each net is kept open by a bar, or beam.

N 86

## Trawler nets

The type of net used by a trawler depends on the type of fish being caught. A beam trawler is used to catch fish on the sea bed, while a purse seine (right) is used to catch a shoal of fish. Purse seining involves dropping a long net around the fish and then closing the net from the bottom, trapping them. Tuna are caught using a long line of hooks.

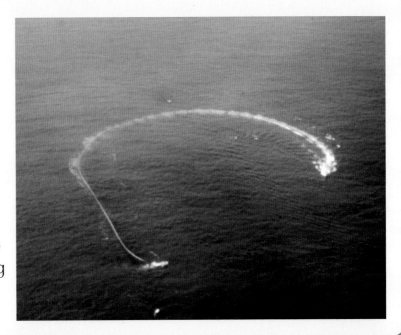

## Cod

The cod is one of the most important fish in the Atlantic. An adult fish grows up to 1.4 metres long and weighs up to 25 kilogrammes. Cod has been overfished (see pages 192–193) and its survival is under threat. In some oceans it is classed as endangered.

Nets of the beam trawler are lowered to the sea bed.

**DID YOU KNOW?** There are as many as four million fishing boats in the world. Each year, they catch about 90 million tonnes of fish.

# Squid

Squid is an important link in the ocean food chain. It is a hunter of smaller animals, such as krill and fish, and is itself the prey of hunters such as swordfish and dolphins.

## Jet propulsion

To move along, a squid draws water into its body and then forces it out through a funnel on its belly. This creates a powerful jet of water that pushes the squid backwards through the water.

Large squid can move at 30 kilometres per hour, faster than many ships can travel.

This squid has caught a fish in its tentacles.

## Tentacles

A squid has eight arms and two longer tentacles. When it gets close to its prey, it shoots out its long tentacles to grab the animal and pull it into its mouth.

Small suckers cover the underside of the arms.

## Colourful messages

Squid can change the colour of their skin. They can blend into the background or change colour to confuse a predator. Their colour reflects their mood too. Angry squid are often red. This squid (left) is bioluminescent – it gives off an eerie glow in the dark.

## Large eye

Squid have large eyes that are very similar to human eyes, with a pupil and a lens. They rely on their sight to find prey.

### DID YOU KNOW?

Squid can die if they become stranded in shallow water. This often happens after they mate and lay their eggs.

# Ocean hunters

Large hunting fish, such as sharks, swordfish and marlin, are at the top of the ocean food chain. These fearsome fish are designed for hunting.

The dorsal fin forms a crest along the back of the fish.

## Marlin

The marlin (right) is related to the tuna and swordfish. It is a large fish with a spear-like snout. It hunts alone, swimming in the surface waters of the ocean in search of fish and squid.

## Swordfish

The swordfish (above) is named after its long, sword-like snout. It does not spear its prey, but moves its "sword" from side to side to slice them up. It swims alone and is often seen leaping out of the water.

## Sailfish

These fish have a large, sail-like fin along their back. They use it to gather together groups of fish and squid, which they then eat. Sailfish can fold back the fin to create a sleek, streamlined shape for swimming.

**DID YOU KNOW?**

Sailfish are the fastest swimming fish. They have an amazing top speed of 110 kilometres per hour.

## Mako shark

The mako is a muscular fish with a tail fin shaped for speed. It can swim at up to 32 kilometres an hour. It has sharp teeth, which it uses to grip slippery prey such as tuna and mackerel.

# Giant fish

Some creatures found in the oceans are huge. These include whales and fish such as basking sharks, disc-shaped sunfish and winged manta rays.

## Manta ray

A manta ray (right) usually swims slowly through the ocean, but when threatened by hunters, such as sharks, it leaps out of the water in an attempt to escape.

The wings of a manta ray can be up to 7 metres wide.

### Ocean-going shark

The white-tipped shark grows to about 4 metres long. It usually swims slowly just below the surface, but sometimes sticks its nose out of the water to sniff the air in search of food.

128

## Wahoo

The wahoo (above) can grow up to 1.7 metres long. It is nicknamed the 'striped rocket' because of its missile-shaped body and its habit of leaping out of the water with its prey in its jaws.

### DID YOU KNOW?

The average length of a sunfish is about 1.8 metres, but some have been found that are 3.2 metres long.

## Sun bather

The sunfish has an unusual shape – it is almost circular when seen from the side, with fins sticking out of the top and bottom of its body. Sunfish feed on jellyfish, and can weigh more than 2000 kilogrammes.

# Ocean turtles

Many turtles make long journeys across the oceans in search of food. They return to the beach where they were born to lay their eggs.

## Growing up

Turtles spend the first few years of their life in the open ocean. They feed on jellyfish and other animals there before returning to coastal waters to mate.

Green turtle

Turtles have flat flippers to help them swim.

## Green turtles

Green turtles are expert swimmers with a smooth, streamlined shell and flippers. They are the largest hard-shelled turtle in the ocean. They grow to a metre across, and weigh 200 kilogrammes or more. Baby green turtles are meat eaters, but adults feed on sea grass.

# Hawksbill turtles

This rare turtle gets its name from the bird-like shape of its head. It spends as long as 20 years at sea before it is ready to breed. Sadly, it is killed for its attractive shell, which is used to make jewellery and ornaments.

# Toothless turtles

All turtles are toothless. Instead of teeth they use their beak to crush coral and crabs, or graze on sea grass. Their head, like the rest of their body, is covered with small scales.

Toothless beak of a hawksbill turtle

## DID YOU KNOW?

Some green turtles feed off the coast of Brazil and swim across the Atlantic to breed on Ascension Island – a round journey of about 4500 kilometres.

131

# Dolphins

The dolphin is one of the most intelligent animals in the ocean. This playful marine mammal uses sound to find its prey, and lives in groups.

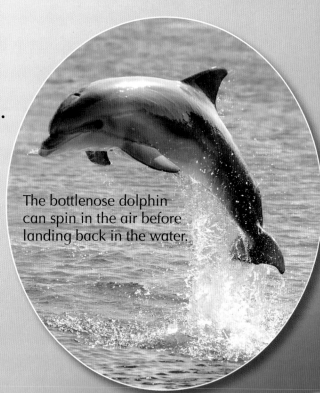

The bottlenose dolphin can spin in the air before landing back in the water.

## Leaping dolphins

The acrobatic dolphin moves its powerful tail up and down to build up enough speed to jump out of the water. Dolphins often leap into the air while chasing fish to eat.

## Hunting with sound

Dolphins use sound to find their prey. This is called echolocation. They make whistling and clicking sounds, which travel through the water. These sounds bounce off any prey in the water, creating echoes that the dolphins can hear.

Sound waves made by dolphin.

Echoes tell the dolphin the shape, size and location of their prey.

## Looking after baby

A female dolphin gives birth to her baby, or calf, under the water. The mother pushes her calf to the surface so it can take its first breath. The calf feeds on its mother's milk for about a year.

## Living together

Dolphins live together in groups called pods. A pod usually contains about 10 to 12 dolphins, but super pods of thousands of dolphins are formed when pods join up.

# Sargasso Sea

The Sargasso Sea is a huge area of floating seaweed in the North Atlantic Ocean. It is home to many animals – some stay all year, but others are just visitors.

Small air sacs keep the sargassum weed afloat.

## Sargassum weed

Thick mats of sargassum weed cover much of the Sargasso Sea. Turtles and fish hide amongst the mats, while crabs and small shrimp cling to the weed.

EUROPE

NORTH AMERICA

Atlantic Ocean

Sargasso Sea

AFRICA

SOUTH AMERICA

## In the mid Atlantic

The Sargasso Sea covers an area of about 3 million square kilometres. It is an area with slow ocean currents surrounded by fast-moving currents.

134

## Seaweed nurseries

The Sargasso Sea is a nursery for many fish. The young of the grey trigger fish (above) drift in the sargassum weed until they reach about 15 centimetres long. Then they swim to coastal reefs.

## Growing eels

Adult eels swim to the Sargasso Sea to lay their eggs. The young eels hatch. They then make their way back to North America and Europe, where they swim up rivers to breed.

**DID YOU KNOW?**

The vast Sargasso Sea is the only sea in the world that does not have a coastline. Instead it is bordered by fast-moving water.

Young eels

# Moving up and down

During the day, the brightly lit surface waters are virtually empty of small animals. Most dive to the safety of the darker water below. At night, it is very different – they all return to feed under the cover of darkness.

## Night-time travellers

This daily movement is only a few hundred metres, but for tiny animals such as shrimps (left) and copepods it is a long journey. It is the only way to feed in safety.

## Mass migration

During the day, most animals living in the open oceans are found at depths of 50 to 1000 metres. At sunset, they swim back to the surface waters. This is one of the largest mass movements of animals in the world.

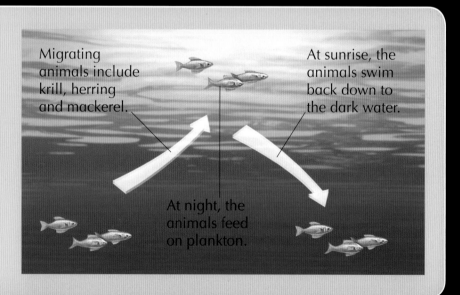

Migrating animals include krill, herring and mackerel.

At sunrise, the animals swim back down to the dark water.

At night, the animals feed on plankton.

Lantern fish travel the greatest distances each day. During daylight, they are found more than 1700 metres down and at night they rise to within 100 metres of the surface.

## Bluefin tuna

The tuna preys on smaller fish, which it swallows whole. It follows its prey on their migration to the deeper water.

# The deep ocean

People have explored the land and the surface
of the oceans, but the deep ocean is still
mysterious. This dark, cold place is the world's
largest habitat, but few people have ventured
into it. The deep ocean is a difficult place
for animals to live in, and for humans to visit.

## Ocean layers

The surface layer goes down to about 200 metres. Next comes the twilight zone, from 200 to 1000 metres. The dark zone stretches to the sea bed.

# Going down

As you descend from the surface, the sea becomes darker and colde The pressure increases, too. In very deep water, a diver would be crushe and all the air squeezed from their lungs. Only animals adapted to this environment can survive.

## Sunlit zone

Sunlight passes through the water to depths of about 200 metres. Here in the surface layer, there is enough light for plant plankton and seaweeds to make their food.

## Twilight zone

Beneath the surface layer, there is a glimmer of light – just enough for some animals to see. Animals dive down from the surface into this layer for safety.

Dolphins spend most of their time in the sunny surface layers.

The sperm whale is an expert diver, spending several hours at a time in the dark zone.

**DID YOU KNOW?** Female sperm whales live in groups, or pods, with their young. Male sperm whales leave the group when they are a few years old to join a group of males.

Brittle stars are found crawling over the sea bed.

## Dark zone

The dark zone is pitch black and cold, and the water is still. Fish and other sea creatures living below 500 metres are designed to withstand the great pressure of the surrounding water.

# Twilight zone

A variety of animals, from tiny plankton to huge whales, live permanently in the twilight zone. Their bodies are specially adapted for life in deep, gloomy water.

## Hatchetfish

A hatchetfish (above) has a flat body. It has light-producing organs on its underside. The lights disguise the fish's shape so it is not spotted by predators in the water below.

## Nautilus

The nautilus is a relative of the squid. It has a spiral shell for protection. If necessary, it can disappear inside completely. Its large eyes help it to see in the gloom.

The nautilus has many more tentacles than a squid, but no suckers.

Eye

142

## Twilight shrimp

The twilight shrimp (right) has a red shell – a colour that is difficult to spot in the gloom. It catches small plankton animals in its claws.

## Fangs in the dark

There is not much food in the twilight zone, so fish make sure that any prey they catch cannot escape. Fish such as this fangtooth have dagger-like teeth that point backwards. This prevents the prey from wriggling out of their mouth.

# Diving deep

Seals, whales, sharks and penguins are just some of the animals that dive down into the twilight zone and beyond to find food.

## Twilight hunter

The sperm whale dives down to 1000 metres, or more, in search of squid. Scientists believe that the whale produces sound waves to stun its prey.

## Diving birds

Many seabirds, such as the penguin, dive underwater to catch food. The penguin is a flightless bird with flippers rather than wings. It is clumsy on land, but an expert swimmer. The emperor penguin spends up to 15 minutes under the water at a time. It dives to depths of about 500 metres.

A sperm whale wrestles with its prey of giant squid.

# Weddell seals

The Weddell seal dives at night to find krill, squid and fish. It can stay under the water for up to an hour, reaching depths of about 700 metres before it has to return to the surface to breathe.

## Megamouth

The odd-looking megamouth shark grows to about 7 metres. It has a metre-wide mouth and a flabby body. Like many ocean animals, it spends the daylight hours in deep water and swims to the surface to feed at night.

**DID YOU KNOW?** Little is known about the megamouth shark, which was first discovered near Hawaii in 1976. Since then, only about 40 megamouths have been seen.

The snipe eel has a row of small backward-facing teeth along its jaws.

# The deep

The deep is a cold, eerie place where very little lives. The animals of the deep have all sorts of unusual features, which help them get something to eat in this 'food desert'.

## Snipe eel

The snipe eel has jaws that do not close. It swims with its mouth open and small animals, such as amphipods (shrimp-like creatures), are trapped on the teeth and swallowed. The snipe eel grows to over a metre long.

## Deep sea medusa

The deep sea medusa (right) is a relative of the jellyfish. It traps prey, such as small shrimp and baby fish, in its long, stinging tentacles.

The gulper eel has a loosely hinged jaw, which it can open very wide.

## Big mouth

Many deep sea fish are all mouth and stomach. The gulper eel has a wide mouth and a very stretchy stomach – it can swallow prey as large as itself.

## Fishing the deep

The angler fish lures its prey with a light that dangles from the end of a spine in front of its large mouth. The light is produced by tiny bacteria.

**DID YOU KNOW?**

It is believed that the *phronima*, a tiny deep sea amphipod, was the model for the monster in the science-fiction film *Alien*.

# Deep sea squid

Many stories have been written about monsters of the deep. One of the most mysterious is the giant squid. These huge animals are rare, and few have been seen alive.

## Historical monster

Many stories have been written about giant squid. In these tales it is said that they have risen from the deep and wrapped their tentacles around boats to pull them down under the water.

## Rare sightings

Sometimes, the bodies of giant squid (above) are washed up on beaches. This gives scientists the chance to study them. Their remains have also been found in the stomachs of sperm whales.

# Light in the dark

Many giant squid (below) can produce their own light. They switch this light on and off to attract fish. When the fish are close enough, the squid grab them.

This deep sea squid, called *Teuthowenia*, produces its own light to attract prey.

**DID YOU KNOW?**

The colossal squid has the largest eyes of any animal. Each eye measures up to 25 centimetres across.

## Colossal squid

The colossal squid is even larger than the giant squid. It is the world's largest invertebrate animal, reaching a massive 14 metres in length. Its tentacles have razor-like hooks, which can cause injuries to other animals.

# Life on the sea bed

Some of the deep sea bed is rocky, but it is mostly covered by a thick layer of mud. This mud contains the remains of dead animals that have dropped from the water above.

## Deep sea spines

The round sea urchin is covered in long spines. Its mouth is on the underside, surrounded by five teeth-like plates. It uses these plates to feed on dead matter and animals such as mussels and sponges.

The round sea urchin can move each of its spines.

## Sea pens

Sea pens (above) are related to corals. Each sea pen is really a colony of individual polyps that live together. The sea pen attaches to the deep sea bed, where it catches small animals with its stinging tentacles.

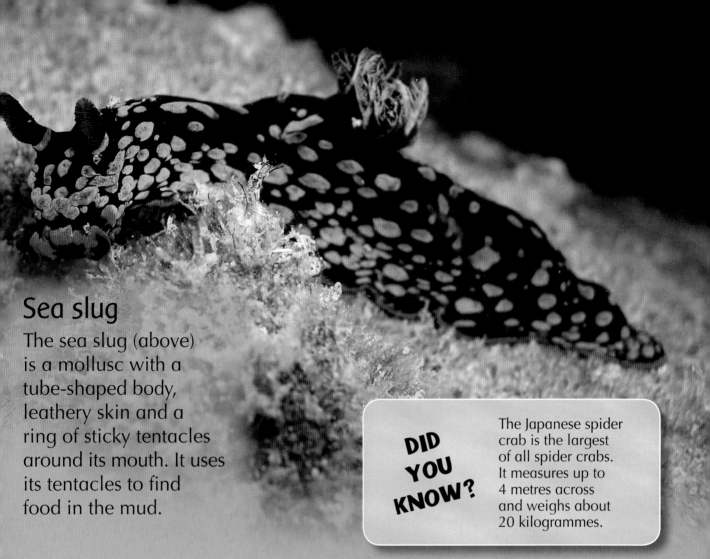

## Sea slug

The sea slug (above) is a mollusc with a tube-shaped body, leathery skin and a ring of sticky tentacles around its mouth. It uses its tentacles to find food in the mud.

## Long-legged crabs

Spider crabs scuttle across the deep sea bed in search of food. They have a small body and 10 very long legs. They cannot see anything in the dark, so they use their sense of touch to catch prey.

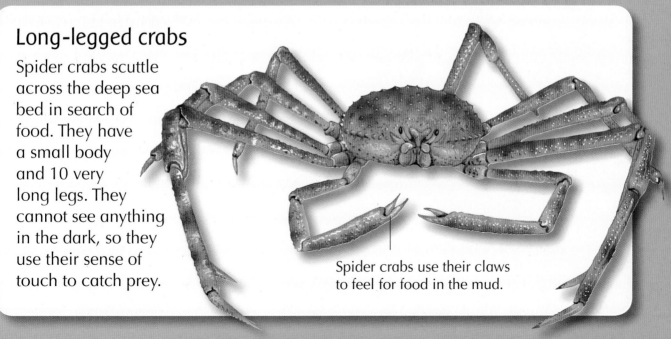

Spider crabs use their claws to feel for food in the mud.

# All sorts of worms

Worms are invertebrate animals with a long, soft, boneless body. There are all sorts of marine worms including tapeworms and fan worms.

## Spaghetti worm

The tentacles of this deep sea worm (right) look a bit like spaghetti. The worm extends these sticky tentacles over the sea bed to catch any small particles that sink down from above.

Hook

Tapeworms use their hooks and suckers to grip to the inside of the gut.

## Undersea parasites

Parasites are animals that live in, and do harm to, other animals. The tapeworm is a common parasite in many deep sea fish. The tapeworm lives and feeds in the fish's gut. Eventually, the fish starves to death.

Sucker

152

## New discovery

Scientists have discovered some new types of worm living on the deep sea bed. These include a type of fan worm (left) that feeds only on the bones of dead whales.

## Catching food

Fan worms are found on the deep sea bed. Their soft body is protected by a hard, bony tube. They extend a ring of sticky tentacles from the top of the tube to catch small animals drifting in the water. If disturbed, fan worms can shoot back inside their tubes.

**DID YOU KNOW?**

More than 400 different types, or species, of animal, including many worms, feed on the bodies of dead whales on the sea bed.

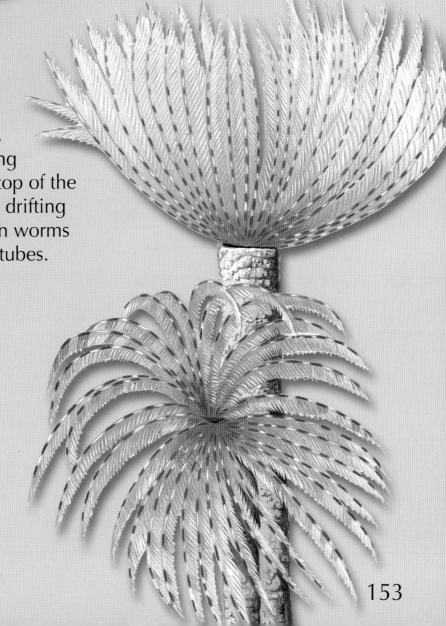

# Food and shelter

When the body of a large animal drops to the sea bed, scavengers come from far and wide to feed upon it. Other animals take shelter among objects that find their way to the sea bed.

## Finding shelter

Animals on the sea bed need shelter from predators. Many hide among bones, or even old cans (below) and other objects that have dropped to the sea bed.

## Food from above

There is a constant supply of 'marine snow' from the waters above. This 'snow' is the broken down remains of dead plants and animals – especially plankton. These remains drift slowly to the sea bed.

## Ocean floor scavenger

The hagfish (above) looks a bit like an eel. It is a scavenger that burrows into the bodies of dead animals – and eats them from the inside out. It is an unusual fish because it does not have jaws or teeth. Instead, it has a very rough tongue.

## Brittle star

The brittle star (right) has five long arms, which it uses to pull itself across the sea bed. It sometimes preys on small shrimps and other animals, but mostly scavenges on dead matter.

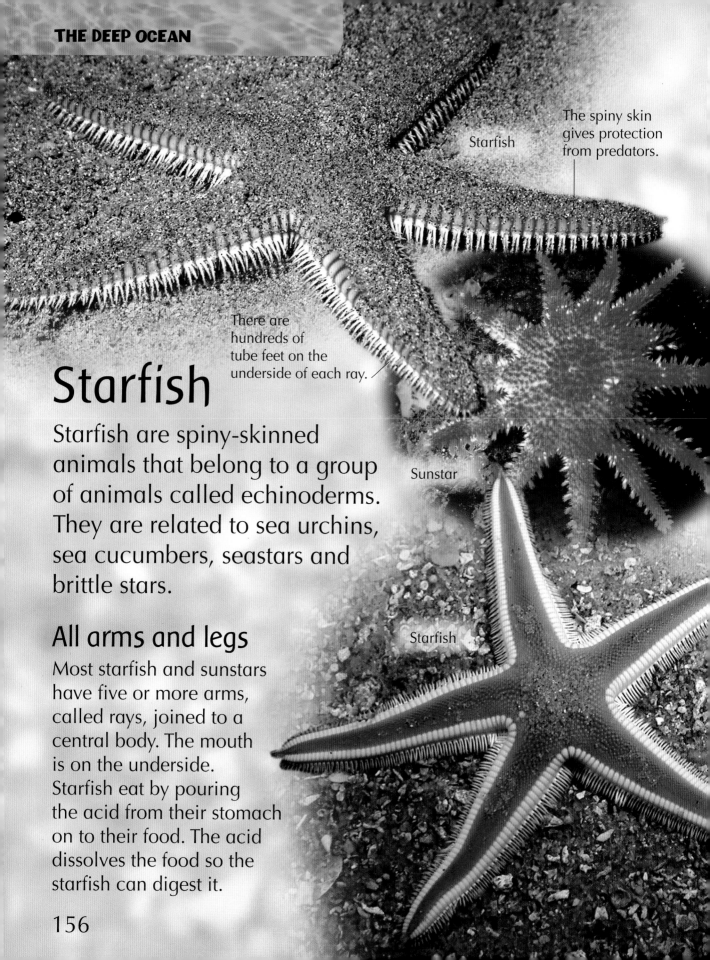

Starfish

The spiny skin gives protection from predators.

There are hundreds of tube feet on the underside of each ray.

Sunstar

Starfish

# Starfish

Starfish are spiny-skinned animals that belong to a group of animals called echinoderms. They are related to sea urchins, sea cucumbers, seastars and brittle stars.

## All arms and legs

Most starfish and sunstars have five or more arms, called rays, joined to a central body. The mouth is on the underside. Starfish eat by pouring the acid from their stomach on to their food. The acid dissolves the food so the starfish can digest it.

# Tube feet

To move, a starfish swings each ray forward then pushes down, pulling itself along. There is a tiny sucker at the end of each ray, to grip. The starfish also uses the sucker to force open the shells of mussels and clams.

## Spare parts

If a starfish loses one of its rays, it can grow a new one. This process is called regeneration. This starfish (below) is regrowing two of its rays.

Mouth

## Sea lilies

Sea lilies, or feather stars, are related to starfish. They have a central mouth surrounded by arms. Some sea lilies are fixed to the sea bed by a stalk, but others can swim.

## DID YOU KNOW?

Sea lilies have survived, almost unchanged, for millions of years. Fossilized sea lilies have been found that are up to 40 metres wide.

157

# Sea bed fish

A surprising number of fish are found on the deep sea bed, and more are being discovered all the time. They have been given unusual names such as the rat-tail, cookie cutter and even the blobfish.

## Deep sea blob

The blobfish (below) was discovered in 2003, on a sea bed 1200 metres deep. Little is known about it, but the shape of its mouth suggests that it eats whatever it can find.

## Six-gill shark

The six-gill shark (right) is found at depths of up to 3000 metres, where it rests during the day. At night, it swims to the surface to hunt for fish and seals. Most sharks have five gill slits, but this shark has six.

Gill slits

## Cookie cutter shark

This shark gets its name from the round scars that it leaves on its prey. It grips its prey in its mouth and, using its long teeth, pulls out a lump of flesh leaving behind a nasty hole.

## Deep sea rat tail

The rat-tail, or grenadier, is one of the most common deep sea fish. It has a large head, a slender body and, unusually, no tail fin. These fish live in water up to 5000 metres deep, where they hunt animals such as smaller fish and shrimps.

## Cliff hugger

Sea anemones, and other animals that cannot swim, cling tightly to the cliff. If they let go, they could sink into the deep below.

A deep-sea crab hides underneath an anemone on a sea cliff.

# Deep ocean cliffs

There are cliffs, mountains and trenches in the deep ocean. These are home to many animals, including corals and sponges.

Deep sea glass sponge

Glass skeleton

## Deep sea sponges

Some deep-water sponges have a skeleton that is made from glass. They produce tiny pieces of glass, which stick together to form a beautiful skeleton that is strong enough to support their body.

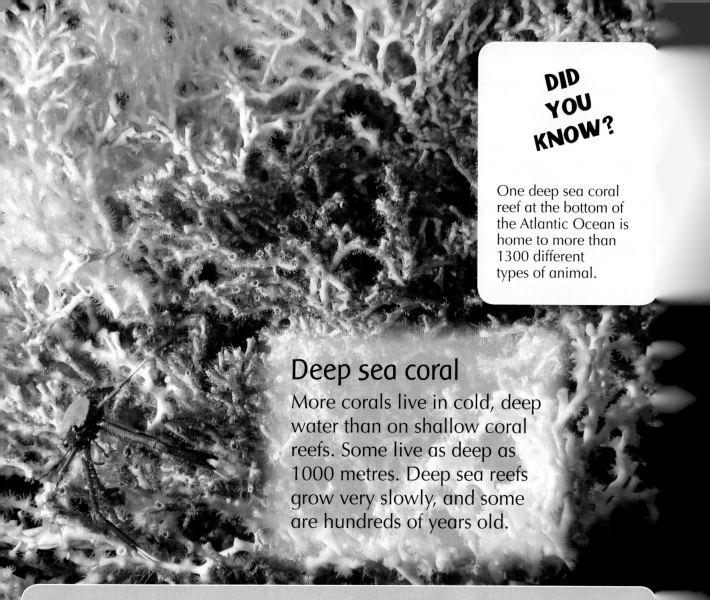

## Deep sea coral

More corals live in cold, deep water than on shallow coral reefs. Some live as deep as 1000 metres. Deep sea reefs grow very slowly, and some are hundreds of years old.

## Hiding in cracks

The wolf fish, or seawolf, pushes its body backwards into the cracks of a cliff. It leaves just its head sticking out, watching for prey. It has a wide mouth with large pointed teeth, which it uses to feed on clams, mussels and starfish.

# Strange new life

In 1976, scientists made an exciting discovery while exploring the deep. They found strange animals, never seen before, clustered around jets of hot water coming out of cracks in the sea bed.

Jet of black water

## Deep sea smokers

The jets of water are often nicknamed black smokers because they look black. The temperature of the water reaches 400 degrees Celsius. A chimney builds up around the jet, formed from minerals in the hot water.

A chimney can reach 60 metres in height, and can grow up to 30 centimetres a day.

**DID YOU KNOW?**

In the Atlantic Ocean huge swarms of shrimp, containing up to 30,000 individuals per square metre, have been found near or on black smokers.

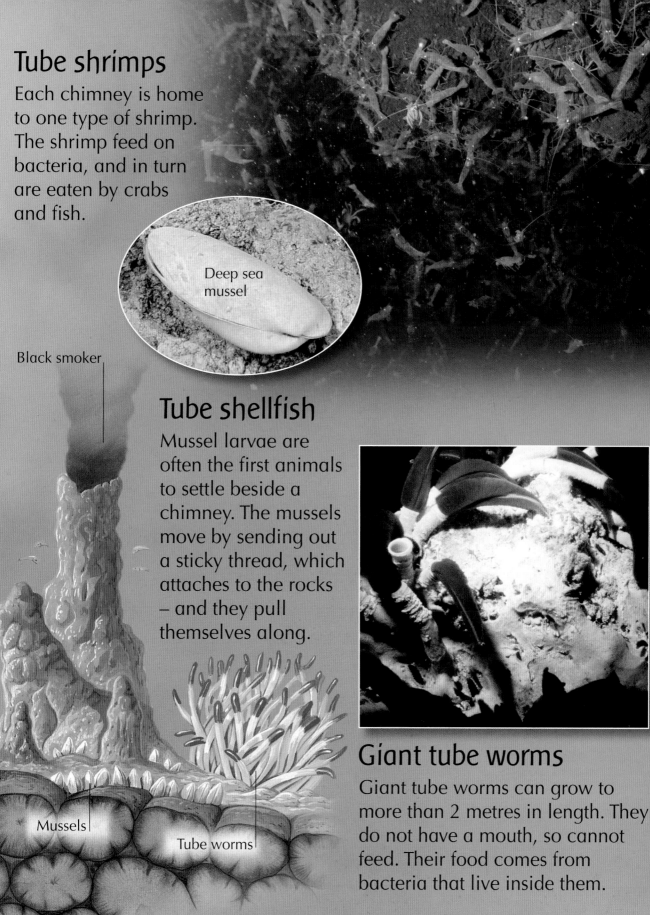

## Tube shrimps

Each chimney is home to one type of shrimp. The shrimp feed on bacteria, and in turn are eaten by crabs and fish.

Deep sea mussel

Black smoker

## Tube shellfish

Mussel larvae are often the first animals to settle beside a chimney. The mussels move by sending out a sticky thread, which attaches to the rocks – and they pull themselves along.

Mussels

Tube worms

## Giant tube worms

Giant tube worms can grow to more than 2 metres in length. They do not have a mouth, so cannot feed. Their food comes from bacteria that live inside them.

# Polar waters

Animals living in the polar regions have to cope with some of the toughest conditions on the planet. The Arctic Ocean surrounds the North Pole. At the South Pole, the continent of Antarctica is covered by a thick sheet of ice. The Southern Ocean surrounds Antarctica, and is also covered by ice for much of the year.

Arctic

# Polar climate

The poles have winters of freezing temperatures, high winds and darkness. In summer, temperatures rise and it stays light all day and all night.

Antarctica

## Ice caps

These maps (left) show the area that is covered by ice all year round. In winter, the areas of ice are even larger.

## Blizzard conditions

Strong polar winds blow snow into the air, creating blizzards. This makes it difficult for animals to move around.

A colony of emperor penguins in a blizzard in Antarctica.

## Midnight sun

At midnight during the polar summer, the Sun does not set. There is enough light to see 24 hours a day. In the winter, the Sun does not rise so it is dark all the time.

This series of photographs was taken of the Arctic summer Sun during the night. It shows that the Sun never sinks below the horizon.

## Lights in the sky

During spring and autumn, strange red, blue and green lights appear in the polar skies. This display is called the aurora borealis in the Arctic. In the Antarctic it is the aurora australis.

**DID YOU KNOW?** At the North and South Poles there is only one full sunrise (where the whole Sun can be seen) and one full sunset (where the whole Sun disappears) each year.

167

# Sea ice

The surfaces of the polar oceans are covered by ice during the winter. As temperatures fall, the sea freezes, forming a thick layer of ice called an ice sheet.

## Sheets of ice

Fresh water freezes at 0 degrees Celsius, but the salt water of the polar oceans freezes at –2 degrees Celsius. The thick sheet of ice formed at the surface is not flat. Strong winds push the sheets of ice together to form ridges.

### Life under the ice

Sea ice forms a protective layer, beneath which live many animals. These include Arctic cod and smaller animals such as krill and copepods. These animals attract hungry predators such as seals (above).

## Growing on ice

Sea ice is not solid like a block of ice. It is criss-crossed with small channels filled with salty water. Tiny living things, such as algae (left), bacteria and copepods, live in these channels. Sometimes there are so many red algae that the ice is coloured red.

## Breaking up ice

In spring, when temperatures rise, the ice sheet breaks up into large chunks called floes. These get smaller and smaller as they are moved around by the ocean currents.

**DID YOU KNOW?**

The Arctic is the least salty ocean in the world. This is because the lack of warm sunshine means that less water evaporates than elsewhere.

Many polar animals, such as seals and penguins, pull themselves out of the water on to the sea ice to rest.

# Icebergs

Icebergs are huge, floating lumps of ice that have broken off ice sheets. They are carried across oceans by winds and currents.

## Under the water

Only about one eighth of an iceberg sticks up above the water (left). The rest is hidden under the water. Icebergs are a danger to ships because sailors cannot see the massive lumps of ice lurking beneath the surface.

## Massive icebergs

In 2005, a huge iceberg broke off the Antarctic ice sheet. It was 120 kilometres long – the largest floating object in the world. It is now blocking the way to the ocean for penguins. This is a problem for the penguins because they have to walk much further over the ice to reach the water to feed.

The large iceberg is stuck across a bay.

Ocean

## Ice islands

Although icebergs look clean and white, they are often covered with a layer of dirt. They can contain rocks, soil and bits of plants. Each year, as many as 40,000 icebergs break off ice sheets in the Arctic. Most drift south into the Atlantic Ocean, where they slowly melt.

## Sunk by an iceberg

On 14 April 1912, a ship called the *Titanic* sank after hitting a huge iceberg in the Atlantic Ocean. The *Titanic* was on its first voyage and was the world's largest ship at the time. Fifteen hundred people died and seven hundred were rescued by other ships.

An iceberg tore a hole in the *Titanic*.

The wreck of the *Titanic* was discovered in 1985.

171

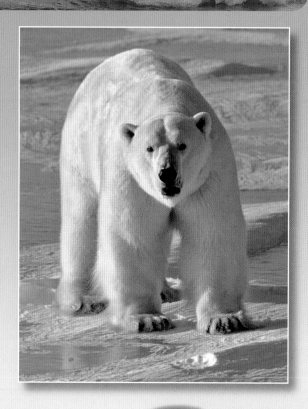

# Living on ice

Animals that live at the poles are adapted to cope with the cold, wind and snow. These include polar bears, Arctic foxes and walruses.

## Prowling the ice

The biggest hunters on the ice are the polar bears (left). Their long claws and furry feet help them to grip on the slippery Arctic surface.

## Polar scavenger

Arctic foxes are scavengers – they eat almost anything they find on the ice. They also hunt small animals. When Arctic foxes hear small rodents, such as voles or lemmings, under the snow, they pounce on them from above. They often bury food to eat later.

The pads of the Arctic fox's feet are covered with thick fur.

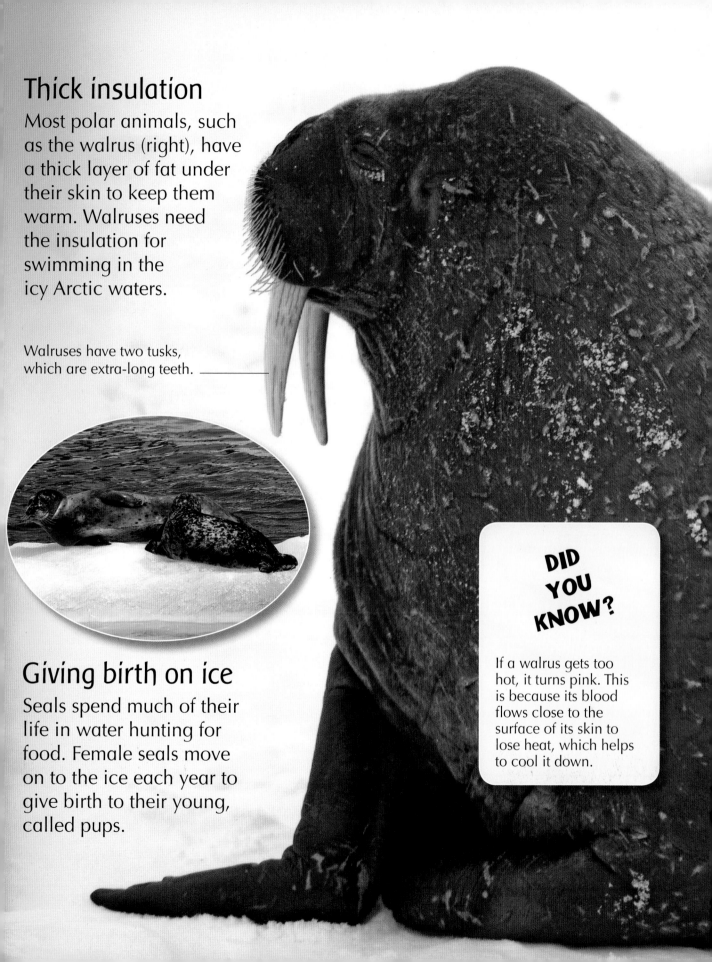

# Thick insulation

Most polar animals, such as the walrus (right), have a thick layer of fat under their skin to keep them warm. Walruses need the insulation for swimming in the icy Arctic waters.

Walruses have two tusks, which are extra-long teeth.

# Giving birth on ice

Seals spend much of their life in water hunting for food. Female seals move on to the ice each year to give birth to their young, called pups.

## DID YOU KNOW?

If a walrus gets too hot, it turns pink. This is because its blood flows close to the surface of its skin to lose heat, which helps to cool it down.

# Under the ice

The polar ice spreads over much of the Arctic and Southern Oceans. Many animals spend their lives under the ice.

## Southern fish

Ice fish live in the deep, cold waters around Antarctica, where they feed on krill and plankton. They grow slowly and live for up to 20 years. Ice fish are caught to be eaten but, sadly, too many have been taken from the ocean and they are now rare.

The ice fish is so called because it looks as though it is made of ice.

## Sea butterfly

The sea butterfly (above) is a type of mollusc without a shell. It has two flaps, or wings, attached to its body, which it uses to move through the water. It feeds on copepods and plankton.

DID YOU KNOW?

Ice fish live in such cold water that they have a special chemical in their blood to stop water from freezing in their body.

174

# Arctic jellyfish

Scientists exploring under the ice have discovered new forms of marine life, including Arctic jellyfish. These large jellyfish feed on plankton and small fish.

This Arctic jellyfish has long tentacles, which can extend for up to 6 metres.

## Arctic cod

Arctic cod like icy water, and are not often seen in warmer water. They grow to 30 centimetres long, and are the favourite food of narwhals and other Arctic whales.

# Penguins

Penguins are birds that do not fly. They are found mostly in the Antarctic and the surrounding islands of the Southern Ocean, where they spend many months at sea.

## Graceful swimmers

Penguins are good swimmers, with a sleek, streamlined body. They use their paddle-like wings to push through the water. They press their feet against their tail, which they use to steer.

## Penguin colonies

Each year, penguins come together to breed. Like seals, they gather in colonies. These groups vary in size from just a few hundred breeding pairs to hundreds of thousands of birds.

A colony of emperor penguins.

# Leaping penguins

Penguins waddle and slide across the ice to the sea before leaping into the water. If they are chased by predators in the water, they swim quickly then leap back on to the safety of the ice.

## Bringing up baby

Both parents look after a chick, taking it in turns to walk to the sea to catch fish. The parent bird stores fish in its stomach, and brings it back up into its mouth to feed the chick.

A chinstrap penguin feeding a chick.

# Seals

Seals are built to survive in polar waters. They have a streamlined body, flippers to help them swim and a thick layer of fat, called blubber, to keep them warm.

## Crabeater seals

There are more crabeater seals (right) in the world than any other seal. There may be as many as 50 million. Despite their name, they do not eat crabs – they feed on krill. Their main predators are leopard seals.

## Seal pups

Seal pups are born on the ice. They feed on their mother's milk, which is high in fat so that they grow very quickly. A harp seal pup can gain as much as 2 kilogrammes in weight each day – that is the same as four bags of sugar.

The white fur of this harp seal pup will change to grey within a few weeks.

## Walruses

Walruses are easily recognized by their two long tusks. They are noisy animals, making a wide range of sounds, such as growls, barks, grunts and clicks – both when they are under the water and above it.

## Coming up for air

Ringed seals (left) can stay under the water for up to 30 minutes, but they have to come to the surface to breathe. When the water starts to freeze over, the seals make breathing holes in the ice, which they keep open throughout the winter.

### DID YOU KNOW?

Hungry polar bears sit next to breathing holes in the ice waiting for a seal to pop out its head.

# Polar whales

Most whales, including the humpback, visit polar waters only to feed. But some whales, such as belugas, spend all year in the chilly Arctic.

## White whale

The beluga (left) is a white whale found in the Arctic. It is very noisy and talks to other belugas using a range of sounds including whistles and squeaks.

## Polar unicorns

Male narwhals have an unusual spiral tusk. The tusk is actually a very long tooth. These whales (right) are rubbing their tusks together. This is not aggression, but is a way of communicating with each other.

180

# Looking for prey

The massive killer whale, or orca (below), hunts in polar waters, feeding on animals such as fish, squid, penguins and seals. Orcas often hunt together. When they see penguins or seals resting on a small ice floe, one orca tips over the ice while the others wait to catch the prey.

The orca is easy to recognize by its black and white markings.

# Trapped by ice

In winter, ice extends quickly over the water and whales that are feeding in bays or between large floes can get trapped. They die if their breathing holes in the ice close up.

## DID YOU KNOW?

In 1978, five humpback whales and one narwhal were trapped by ice in a bay in Newfoundland, Canada. For two months, people kept breathing holes open for the whales until the ice melted and they could escape.

# Polar bears

Polar bears are the largest hunters of the Arctic. Their white fur is good camouflage against the white snow. Their excellent senses help them to find prey on the ice.

## Polar hunter

Polar bears are at the top of the Arctic food chains. They have no enemies other than people. They feed mainly on seals, but also eat birds, fish and small mammals.

Polar bears paddle with their front paws and steer with their hind legs.

## Champion swimmer

Polar bears are strong swimmers and can swim huge distances. They often have to swim between ice floes when the ice starts to break up in spring.

## Scavenging

A dead whale washed up on a beach provides a feast for polar bears. Polar bears live alone, but large numbers will gather each day to feed on a dead whale.

## Polar cubs

Female polar bears usually give birth to two cubs. The mother lives in a den under the ice and snow in winter, where her cubs are born. In the spring, mother and cubs emerge to find food.

# Albatrosses

Albatrosses spend much of their lives at sea, gliding over the Southern and Pacific Oceans in search of fish.

## Gliding over the waves

The long wings of the albatross are the perfect shape for catching the wind and gliding. Albatrosses cover huge distances – some types fly more than 1000 kilometres in just one day.

## Polar nests

Most albatrosses breed once every two years. They return to land to nest on rocky cliffs and coastal slopes. The females lay a single egg that hatches several months later.

The wandering albatross has the largest wingspan of any bird, reaching up to 3.5 metres. Each wing is almost as wide as an adult human being is tall.

## Albatross chicks

Both parents care for the albatross chick, feeding it with fish and squid for up to 7 months. An albatross is ready to breed when it is about 10 years old, and lives for up to 60 years.

## Hook bill

An albatross's bill is up to 18 centimetres long, with a hook at the end. The bird swoops down to the surface of the water and catches slippery fish and squid in its large bill.

Arctic tern

## Speedy fliers

Arctic terns fly further than any other birds. They spend half of the year in the Arctic, where they lay their eggs and raise young. The parent birds and all their young then fly south to the Antarctic for rest of the year.

# Summer visitors

Arctic winters are harsh, but long summer days attract lots of animals. Birds spend the summer here feeding and raising their young. In autumn, they fly away to warmer places.

## Greylag geese

Greylag geese (left) are large geese with grey-brown feathers and pink legs. They are so-called because they lag behind other birds and are often the last geese to fly north in spring.

186

## Snow geese

Flocks of snow geese (above) fly north each spring. They leave their winter feeding grounds in the USA to return to the Arctic. Snow geese are white with black wing tips.

Whooper swan

## Whooper swans

Whooper swans breed in Northern Europe and Iceland. Individual birds can be identified from the black markings on the bill because each bird has different markings.

**DID YOU KNOW?**

Arctic terns live for about 20 years and will fly more than 800,000 kilometres in their lifetime. That is further than flying to the Moon and back.

# Living and working at the poles

Some people have lived in the Arctic for many generations and others, such as scientists, have moved there to work. The only people who live in the Antarctic are scientists.

## Surviving on ice

Hunters spend many weeks on the Arctic ice hunting for food. They build a domed shelter, called an igloo (above), from blocks of ice. It is warm inside the igloo as the ice traps body heat.

## Traditional life

In the past, native people such as the Inuit (left) relied on the sea for food and on animal skins to make clothes. They cut up and dried fish so it could be eaten all winter, when the sea was frozen and it was not possible to fish.

# Polar fishing

The polar waters are full of fish. Throughout the summer months, when the ice melts, many fishing boats sail into the region. The boats catch fish, squid and shellfish such as crabs and prawns.

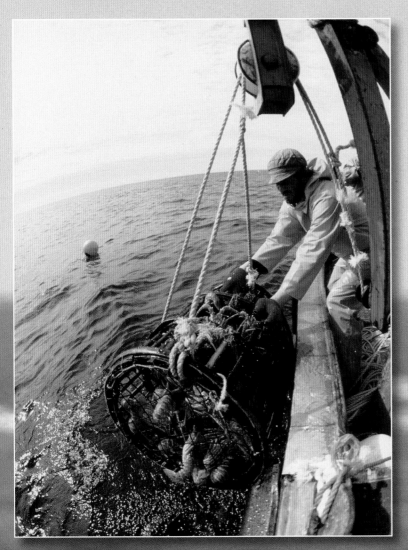

**DID YOU KNOW?**

About 4000 scientists live in the Antarctic during the summer, but fewer than 1000 spend the long, cold winter there.

## Studying polar life

Many scientists are based in the Arctic and Antarctic, studying the animals and the polar environment. These scientists (right) have caught and tagged a Weddell seal so that they can track its movements.

# Oceans in danger

People use the oceans to transport goods around the world, as a source of food and even as a dumping ground for all sorts of waste. Sadly, people are damaging the world's oceans. This damage is caused by over-fishing, pollution and global warming.

# Over-fishing

Fish is an important source of food for many people. As the world's population grows, more fish, squid, prawns and other sea foods are being caught.

## Hauling in the nets

Trawlers drag huge nets that can catch tonnes of fish at a time. 'Purse seine' nets are designed to trap whole shoals, while long lines of hooks catch thousands of fish at the surface or on the sea bed.

## Fishing fleet

These fishing boats, called trawlers, use modern equipment to find shoals of fish. However, large trawlers use lots of energy. It takes twice as much fuel to catch a tonne of fish as it did 20 years ago because fish stocks are lower and boats have to travel further to find them.

Over-fishing using trawlers like this disrupts the ocean food chains. Not enough fish is left behind for marine animals to eat.

## Fish fingers

Some fish are processed on board. The fish are cleaned, gutted and boned, leaving a piece of fish meat called a fillet. This can be sold as fresh fish, or made into processed foods such as fish fingers.

## Catching sharks

Sharks are caught for their meat and fins, which are used in shark fin soup. Often, the fins are cut off and the sharks are thrown back into the water, where they die. Sharks grow slowly and do not reproduce quickly. Too many are being caught and some species may die out.

# Farming fish

Fish have been farmed in some parts of the world for thousands of years. Farming fish can help to save the world's wild fish, but only if it is done carefully.

## Feeding fish

Farmed fish are fed a diet containing all the nutrients they need for healthy growth. The fish grow quickly and, when they are the right size, they are taken to market.

A worker feeds salmon at a fish farm in Maine, USA.

A salmon farm in Scotland

## Salmon farms

Salmon are raised in large, floating cages (above) along the coasts of countries such as Scotland and Norway. The salmon can swim about in the cage, but they cannot escape.

## Trout farming

Trout are also raised on fish farms. There can be problems with farmed fish. Diseases spread quickly, and the fish may have to be treated with chemicals, which can cause pollution.

Salmon

Trout

A prawn pond in Thailand.

## Prawn ponds

Prawn farming is common along tropical coastlines. Mangrove swamps are cleared to make way for prawn farms. This upsets the local food chain, and endangers plants and animals.

A cooked prawn.

**DID YOU KNOW?** Each year, salmon farms around the world produce more than a million tonnes of fish.

# Fish conservation

Overfishing means that too many fish are being taken from the world's oceans. There are several ways in which people can fish that protect future stocks.

## Protected breeds

One way to protect fish is to ban fishing in areas where endangered fish species breed. This gives young fish a chance to survive to adulthood so that they can breed.

## Fishing bans

When fishermen started using 'purse seine' nets, they caught whole shoals of herring. Fishing in the North Sea was banned for a while to allow herring stocks to recover, but there are still not as many as there used to be.

# Fish markets

There are good stocks of some types of fish, such as coley. People can help to protect endangered species by choosing to eat these fish rather than those such as Atlantic cod or Patagonian tooth fish, which are dying out.

## Checking nets

Fishermen can use nets with larger holes, so that smaller, younger fish can escape and only the larger, older fish are caught.

A fishermen checking a net.

197

# Ocean transport

Ships of all kinds carry people and goods around the world. Huge container ships carry goods, tankers are full of oil and cruise ships have thousands of passengers on board.

## Propeller dangers

Sometimes, marine animals and boats crash into each other. Animals can be badly injured by the propeller blades at the back of a boat. Many manatees (right), for example, have been harmed by tourist boats getting too close.

### Sonar confusion

Some scientists believe that booming sounds made by submarines can confuse marine mammals such as whales and dolphins. The animals may swim into shallow water and become stranded on beaches.

A manatee inspects a propeller off the coast of Florida, USA.

# Shipwreck

Sometimes, cargo ships sink during storms or after collisions and their load falls into the sea. The *MS Napoli* (right) broke up off the south coast of England in 2007. Its containers were washed up on to nearby beaches.

Containers from the *Napoli* washed up on the coast of southern England.

# Oil spills

Tankers transport millions of tonnes of oil across the world's oceans. There have been many accidents involving oil tankers where spilt oil ends up in the water.

## Tanker wreck

In 1993, the *Braer* was stranded in shallow water off the coast of Shetland. The wind and waves carried oil along the coast and on to nearby beaches.

## Cleaning the shore

It is difficult to clean an oily beach. Tractors are needed to dig up the oily sand, and rocks have to be pressure-cleaned with powerful jets of water. Sometimes it is better to let the oil break down naturally.

Oil pours out of the *Braer* tanker, on to the surface of the water.

# Wildlife under threat

Any bird, mammal, fish or other animal that swims into an oil slick gets covered in the thick oil. It sticks to the birds' feathers and animals' fur, and blocks fishes' gills. Many die straight away, but a few may be rescued.

## Helping animals

Birds try to clean the oil off their feathers and end up swallowing it. Oily birds are taken to rescue centres, where they are cleaned and cared for until they are well enough to be released.

**DID YOU KNOW?**

One of the worst oil spills happened in 1989, when the *Exxon Valdez* leaked 10 million tonnes of oil into the sea around Alaska. Up to 500,000 birds, 5000 sea otters, 250 bald eagles and many salmon, whales and seals died.

# Dumping ground

Over the years, people have dumped lots of waste, such as rubbish, chemicals and sewage, in the world's oceans. Tides carry the waste away out of sight, but it still harms marine animals.

## Killing fish

Fish need clean water full of oxygen so that they can breathe. Fish living in coastal waters can be harmed by sewage, fertilizers and chemicals emptied into the sea. Extra nutrients caused by sewage and fertilizers can increase bacteria growth. This uses up all the oxygen in the water, so the fish die.

## Polluting sewage

Millions of litres of sewage (left) are emptied into the oceans each year. Some of it is treated, but a lot is raw. Raw sewage looks and smells horrible when it washes back on to beaches. It also contains harmful bacteria that cause disease.

## Rubbish hazards

Rubbish often sinks to the sea bed, where ocean creatures can be tangled. It also washes up on beaches, where it can harm birds and animals.

## Waste by sea

Many countries have strict rules about the ways in which rubbish is dealt with on land. The rules for dumping waste from ships (above) far out at sea are less strict.

# Dangers to animals

A rubbish-clearing boat in France.

Each year, hundreds of thousands of animals die because of rubbish in the oceans. Some die after eating the rubbish, while others are trapped in old fishing nets and lines.

## Cleaning up

The tides wash rubbish on to beaches all around the world. Recently, volunteers found more than 370,000 pieces of litter on 187 kilometres of British beaches. Special boats are used in some areas to scoop rubbish out of the sea before it is washed ashore.

## Floating rubbish

Floating plastic bags look a bit like jellyfish, and are eaten by dolphins, whales and turtles. The bags can block animals' guts and cause them to starve and die.

A spinner dolphin playing with a plastic bag.

# Killer nets

Some of the largest fishing nets are many kilometres long. They hang like curtains in the ocean. As well as fish, they catch dolphins, whales, sharks and turtles. These animals can become tangled in the nets and die.

## DID YOU KNOW?

In 2002, a minke whale was found dead on a beach in France. It had 800 kilogrammes of plastic bags in its stomach.

# Freeing trapped animals

Divers around the world help to save trapped animals such as turtles, dolphins and even whales. They cut them free from the nets so they can swim away.

Freed turtle

A diver frees a turtle that was trapped in a shrimp net.

# Whaling

Many species of whale are protected today, but this has not always been the case. For hundreds of years people hunted whales for their meat and oil, and some species almost died out.

## Whaling today

In 1986, some countries agreed to ban whaling. It was decided, however, that some native people could still hunt and kill whales, and some could also be killed for scientific purposes. Countries such as Japan and Iceland want to start whale hunting again.

A picture of whaling ships from the 1800s.

## Whaling in the past

There was a huge increase in whaling in the 1840s. People used a weapon called a harpoon to kill the whales. More than 40,000 whales were caught each year. By the 1970s, there were fewer than 6000 whales left in the oceans.

## Whaling protests

Many people think whaling is wrong, and organizations such as Greenpeace lead protests against it. Greenpeace boats (right) try to stop whaling boats from catching whales.

# Herding whales

Each year, the people of the Faroe Islands carry out a pilot whale hunt. They drive the whales into bays using boats, and kill them in shallow water. Some local people eat the meat and say the hunt is part of their culture. Others want it stopped.

Dead whales lie on a beach in the Faroe Islands.

A dead whale is dragged ashore in the Madeira Islands in 1972, before whale hunting was banned.

## DID YOU KNOW?

Since the ban in 1986, almost 27,300 whales have been killed. Many of these have been killed by Japanese whaling boats – for scientific purposes.

Whale shark

## Changing habits

As the sea gets warmer, some marine animals change their behaviour. They appear in places where they have not been seen before. As coral reefs die (see pages 210–211), some sharks may have to look elsewhere for food.

# Global warming

Global warming is the gradual increase in the temperature of the Earth's surface. Scientists believe this will cause climates to change, sea levels to rise and extreme weather to become more common.

**DID YOU KNOW?**

As oceans warm up ice melts, the water expands and sea levels rise. Sea levels have increased by as much as 25 centimetres over the last 100 years.

## Smaller hunting grounds

Warmer weather is causing the Arctic ice to melt earlier each year. This causes problems for polar bears (right). The bears hunt on the ice and, if it melts, they are not able to catch enough food and may starve.

Polar bears

A power station releasing greenhouse gases.

## Polluting the atmosphere

Global warming is thought to be caused by an increase in greenhouse gases such as carbon dioxide. These gases trap heat in the atmosphere. Carbon dioxide is produced when oil, gas and coal are burnt.

## How we can help

Everybody can help to slow down global warming by walking and cycling as this does not burn oil. If we travel in aeroplanes, buses or cars carbon dioxide is produced, which may speed up global warming.

209

# Saving coral reefs

Coral reefs are fragile habitats that are easily damaged. They are under threat from global warming, water pollution and over-fishing.

## Killing coral

Corals like warm seas but, if the temperature increases, the organisms living in the corals leave and the corals turn white and die (below). This is called bleaching.

A motorbike on the wreck of *SS Thistlegorm* in the Red Sea.

## Clearing reefs

Like beaches, coral reefs can also become covered in rubbish. Divers can help to conserve the reefs by removing plastic bags, glass bottles, cans and other rubbish.

## Creating new reefs

Ship wrecks are soon covered in corals and other reef animals. New reefs can be created by sinking old ships, cars and tanks in warm, shallow water.

## Making a new home

This squirrel fish (below) is hiding in a pipe on an artificial reef. The rough surfaces help sponges and corals to become attached.

**DID YOU KNOW?**

The world's largest artificial reef was created when the aircraft carrier *USS Oriskany* was sunk off the coast of Florida in 2006.

Squirrel fish

211

# Using ocean power

One way to stop global warming is to use renewable sources of energy, such as the Sun, wind and water instead of coal, oil and gas. Oceans offer a source of wind, wave and tidal power.

## Wind power at sea

It is often windy at sea, so wind farms (right) can be built in shallow water near coasts. Electricity created by wind turbines is carried to the shore by underwater cables.

## Wave power

Waves smash against the coasts with great energy. In this wave power station (above), water is forced along a narrow channel. This spins a turbine, which generates electricity.

## Effects on bird life

Great care has to be taken when choosing where to build offshore wind farms. They must not be built too close to seabird colonies or on bird migration routes.

## Effects on sea life

It is important to make sure that wave power stations and wind farms do not harm the habitats of marine animals such as porpoises (above) or damage the sea bed.

This wind farm is off the coast of Denmark.

# Protecting oceans

There are many ways to protect oceans. Beaches where turtles and other marine animals breed can be safe-guarded. International laws can protect whales and dolphins, and coral reefs can be made into nature reserves.

## Studying the oceans

There is a lot to learn about the world's oceans. People have only just started to explore the deepest parts. By studying the oceans scientists will be able to find ways of protecting them for the future.

## Ocean parks

Important areas of the oceans, such as coral reefs and fish breeding grounds, can be made into marine nature reserves. Here, all animals and plants are protected and fishing is banned.

## A helping hand

Many baby turtles die on beaches before they even reach the sea. One way to make sure more survive is to collect turtle eggs (right) and keep them safe until the tiny turtles hatch. The baby turtles are then taken straight out to sea.

## Eco-tourism

People love to watch whales and dolphins, and to dive on coral reefs. By protecting ocean life, local people may be able to earn money from tourism rather than from industries that harm the environment.

**DID YOU KNOW?**

The world's largest marine reserve is being planned. It will stretch for more than 2200 kilometres along a chain of islands, north of the Hawaiian Islands in the Pacific.

# Some useful words

**☾ Abyss**
The very bottom of the deep ocean, usually deeper than 1755 metres.

**☾ Bill**
The beak of a bird.

**☾ Bird**
A warm-blooded animal with a body covered in feathers, and with wings instead of arms. Female birds lay eggs.

**☾ Bivalve**
A mollusc that has two shells that are hinged together.

**☾ Camouflage**
A special colouring and body shape that blends with the surroundings so that an animal is not spotted easily by either predators or prey.

**☾ Carcass**
The dead body of an animal.

**☾ Carnivore**
An animal that eats other animals.

**☾ Colony**
A group of animals living together.

**☾ Creek**
A small stream.

**☾ Crest**
The very top of a wave.

**☾ Cylindrical**
Tube-shaped.

**☾ Debris**
The remains of something that has been broken into pieces.

**☾ Environment**
The wider surroundings in which an animal or plant lives.

**☾ Equator**
An imaginary line that runs around the Earth's surface, halfway between the two poles.

**☾ Estuary**
A place where a river meets the sea and where salt water from the sea mixes with the fresh water of the river.

**☾ Fin**
A part of the body of a fish that is used for swimming.

## Frond
The leaf-like part of a seaweed.

## Gill
The parts of the body used by fish and some other animals to allow them to breathe underwater.

## Graze
Eat grasses and other plants.

## Habitat
The name given to the place where an animal or plant lives.

## Horizon
The line in the distance that appears to separate the sky from the sea or land.

## Hydrothermal vents
Places on the deep sea bed where super-hot water gushes out of gaps in the rocks.

## Iceberg
A floating mass of ice.

## Invertebrate
An animal that does not have a backbone.

## Lagoon
An area of salty water cut off from the sea by a bank of shingle, sand or coral.

## Larva
The growing stage of an animal such as a young fish or squid.

## Mammal
A warm-blooded animal. Female mammals give birth to live young and feed them with their own milk.

## Mangrove
Trees that grow along muddy coastlines in warm parts of the world.

## Marine
To do with the sea.

## Microscopic
Too small to be seen with the naked eye.

## Migration
A regular journey made by an animal, sometimes over very long distances.

## Mollusc
An animal with a soft body, usually protected by an outer shell.

## Moult
Lose hair, feathers or a shell in order to grow new ones.

## Nursery
A place where young animals live while they are growing up.

## Nutrient
A substance that is needed for healthy growth and living.

## Organism
A living thing such as an animal, plant, fungus or bacterium.

## Plankton
The tiny plants and animals that are found floating close to the surface of ponds, lakes and seas.

## Polar
To do with the areas around the North and South Poles.

## Population
The number of individuals living in a particular area.

## Predator
An animal that hunts and feeds on other animals.

## Prey
An animal that is hunted by other animals.

## Reptile
A cold-blooded animal with a backbone and scaly skin that lays its eggs on dry ground.

## Reproduce
Breed, or have babies.

## Scale
A small, plate-like structure that is found on the skin of reptiles and fish.

## Scavenger
An animal that feeds on the bodies of dead animals.

## Sedentary
Staying in one place or area without moving.

## Sewage
The watery waste from toilets.

## Sextant
A mechanical instrument, mainly used in the past by sailors. It is used to measure the postion of the Sun, Moon or stars. From this, sailors can work out where they are.

## Shingle
Gravel and small stones.

## Shingle bank
A pile of shingle washed onto a beach.

## Shoal
A group of fish that swim together.

## Solitary

A plant or animal that lives alone.

## Sonar

A way of finding the position of objects or prey by using sound waves that travel through the water.

## Spawn

Release lots of small eggs as fish, molluscs or frogs do.

## Structure

The way something is built or put together.

## Stun

Shock or knock out.

## Tentacle

A long, feeler-like structure found on certain animals, such as jellyfish, anemones and squid.

## Titanium

A silvery grey metal.

## Tornado

A powerful spinning column of air that forms from a storm cloud and is very destructive.

## Vertebrate

An animal that has a backbone.

## Wading

Walking in shallow water.

# Index

# Acknowledgments

Artwork supplied by Peter Bull, The Art Agency.

Photo credits:
b = bottom, t = top, r = right, l = left, c = centre

Cover images:
Front: br Frank Krahmer/Getty Images, bc Don Farrall/Getty Images, cc Frank Greenaway/Getty Images, tc AFP/Getty Images, l Stephen Frink/Getty Images.
Back: bc Frank Greenaway/Getty Images, bl James Balog/Getty Images.
Spine: Steve Gorton/Getty Images.

1 Dreamstime.com/Mikhail Blajenov, 2-3 Stephen Frink/Corbis, 4-5 Stuart Westmorland/Corbis, 6tl Dreamstime.com/Nikolay Alexandrov, 6tr Dreamstime.com, 6c Dreamstime.com, 6bl Dreamstime.com/John Abramo, 6br Dreamstime.com, 7t istockphoto.com/Tore Johannesen, 7b Dreamstime.com/David Lloyd, 8–9 Stuart Westmorland/Corbis, 10tl Dreamstime.com/Jan Will, 11tr Dreamstime.com/Wolfgang Amri, 11b Dreamstime.com/Matthias Weinrich, 12tr Bettmann/CORBIS, 12b Dreamstime.com, 13bl istockphoto.com/ Adam Booth, 12bm National Archive of Canada, 14t Dreamstime.com, 14-15b istockphoto.com, 15t Goebel/zefa/Corbis, 15m Dreamstime.com/Lucila De Avila, 16tl Dreamstime.com, 17t Dreamstime.com/Caroline Henri, 17b Dreamstime.com/Mark Ross, 18b Dreamstime.com/Peter Elvidge, 19b Dreamstime.com, 20-21 Dreamstime.com/Matthew Scholey, 20cl NASA, 21tr Harish Tyagi/epa/Corbis, 21b NOAA, 22l Dreamstime.com/Simon Gurney, 22b Digital Vision, 23tl Digital Vision, 23b Digital Vision, 24-25t Dreamstime.com/Ian Scott, 24b Dreamstime.com/Stacy Barnett, 25tr Dreamstime.com/Cathy Figuli, 25b Dreamstime.com/Andrea Leone, 26bl Dreamstime.com, 27t Chris & Monique Fallows/OceanwideImages.com, 27bl Dreamstime.com/Miguel Angelo Silva, 27br Dreamstime.com/Laurin Rinder, 28cl Dreamstime.com/Jan Martin Will, 28br Dreamstime.com/Igor Groshev, 29t Dreamstime.com/John Stublar, 30tr Dreamstime.com/Linda Bucklin, 30b Dreamstime.com/Nick Poling, 31tl Dreamstime.com/Simon Gurney, 31b Stephen Frink/Corbis, 32tl Ralph White/CORBIS, 32b Ralph White/CORBIS, 33m all NOAA, 34-35 Martin Harvey/Corbis, 36l Dreamstime.com/Anna Karwowska, 36br Dreamstime.com/Peter Clark, 37t Dreamstime.com/Joe Gough, 37b NASA, 38t istockphoto.com, 38b Dreamstime.com/Publicimage, 39tl Dreamstime.com, 39r Dreamstime.com/Michael Johnson Jr, 40t Dreamstime.com/Stuart Key, 40b Dreamstime.com/Jay Prescott, 41t Bob Rowan; Progressive Image/CORBIS, 41b Dreamstime.com, 42-43 Dreamstime.com/ImagecD.co.uk, 42b Dreamstime.com/Jesse, 43t Dreamstime.com/Darryl Sleath, 43b Dreamstime.com/Gail Johnson, 44-45 Dreamstime.com/Mikhail Matsonashvili, 44br Dreamstime.com/Dmitry Pichugin, 45t Dreamstime.com/Elena Elisseeva, 45b Dreamstime.com/Nikolay Dimitrov, 46tl Dreamstime.com, 46br Lawson Wood/CORBIS, 47b Stuart Westmorland/CORBIS, 48-49 Dreamstime.com/Robert Adrian Hillman, 48b Dreamstime.com/Nico Smit, 49t Robin Williams; Ecoscene/CORBIS, 49b Dreamstime.com/Randy Harris, 50l NASA, 50b Yann Arthus-Bertrand/CORBIS, 51t Dreamstime.com/Sandy Matzen, 51b Dreamstime.com, 52b Dreamstime.com/Stefan Ekernas, 53t Dreamstime.com/Dragoneye, 53b Dreamstime.com/Heather Jones, 54t Dreamstime.com/Dmitrijs Mihejevs, 54b Dreamstime.com/Emilia Kun, 55t Marco Schmidt, 55b Dreamstime.com/Stefan Ekernas, 56-57 Dreamstime.com/Daniel Gustavsson, 56b Dreamstime.com/Anthony J. Hall, 57t Dreamstime.com/Jeff Gynane, 57b Dreamstime.co/Anthony Hall, 58t Dreamstime.com, 58b Paulo Whitaker/Reuters/Corbis, 59t Dreamstime.com/Jessica Fitzel, 59cl Roger Garwood and Trish Ainslie/CORBIS, 59br Dreamstime.com/Steffen Foerster, 60-61 Stephen Frink/Corbis, 62cl Visuals Unlimited/ Corbis, 63tl Douglas P. Wilson; Frank Lane Picture Agency/CORBIS, 63r NASA, 64 cl Uwe Kils, 65tr istockphoto.com, 65b NOAA, 66tl Brandon D. Cole/CORBIS, 66bc NOAA, 66-67b istockphoto.com/ Klaas Lingbeek-van Kranen, 67t Dreamstime.com/Harald Bolten, 68b Dreamstime.com/Bernard Beton, 69t Dreamstime.com/Jan Will, 69b NOAA, 70tl Dreamstime.com, 70-71 Dreamstime.com, 71tl Dreamstime.com, 71tc Dreamstime.com, 71tr Dreamstime.com/Marcel Nijhuis, 71br Dreamstime.com/Radu Razvan, 72l and bc Dreamstime.com/Jeff Waibel, 73l Jeffrey L. Rotman/CORBIS, 73tr Dreamstime.com/Chris Ryan, 73br Dreamstime.com, 74c istockphoto.com, 74bl Dreamstime.com, 75tl istockphoto.com, 75 Dreamstime.com, 76-77 Stuart Westmorland/Corbis, 76bl Dreamstime.com/Dejan Sarman, 77bl Jeffrey L. Rotman/CORBIS, 77r Dreamstime.com/Steffen Foerster, 78bl Dreamstime.com/Fotograf77, 78-79 Dreamstime.com/David Lloyd, 79cl Dreamstime.com/Anita Huszti, 79br istockphoto.com, 80tl DK Limited/CORBIS, 80cr Dreamstime.com/Ken Moore, 80b Dreamstime.com/Eric Isselée, 81b Dreamstime.com/Brett Atkins, 82cl istockphoto.com/Sandra Minarik, 82b istockphoto.com, 83t istockphoto.com/Adam White, 83bl Theo Allofs/Corbis, 84tr CORBIS SYGMA, 84bl istockphoto.com, 84br Wolfgang Kaehler/CORBIS, 85t istockphoto.com, 86-87 Stuart Westmorland/Corbis, 88-89t istockphoto.com, 89bl Dreamstime.com/Chinieh, 89cr Dreamstime.com/Duard Van Der Westhuizen, 90tl NOAA, 90b Dreamstime.com/ Asther Lau Choon Siew, 91t Dreamstime.com/John Abramo, 91b Dreamstime.com/John Anderson, 92cr NASA, 93tl Dreamstime.com, 93r Dreamstime.com/Holger Wulschlaeger, 94tr istockphoto.com, 94b Dreamstime.com/Asther Lau choon siew, 95t Dreamstime.com/Asther Lau choon siew, 95b Jeffrey L. Rotman/CORBIS, 96t Dreamstime.com, 96b istockphoto.com/Adam Schneider, 97 istockphoto.com, 97br Dreamstime.com/Dirk-jan Mattaar, 98t Dreamstime.com/Andrea Leone, 98bl Brandon D. Cole/CORBIS, 99tr Stephen Frink/CORBIS, 99b istockphoto.com, 100tr and 101tr Dreamstime.com/Mikhail Blajenov, 100bl istockphoto.com/Dan Schmitt, 101tl Dreamstime.com/Asther Lau choon siew, 101br David Burdick, 102t Dreamstime.com, Beverly Speed, 102tl Dreamstime.com/Asther Lau choon siew, 102bl Dreamstime.com/Cornelis Opstal, 103t Dreamstime.com/Wei Send Chen, 103br istockphoto.com/ Dan Schmitt, 104cr Dreamstime.com/Olga Khoroshunova, 104b NOAA, 105t istockphoto.com/Chris Dascher, 105b Douglas P. Wilson; Frank Lane Picture Agency/CORBIS, 106tr istockphoto.com/RbbrDckyBK, 106b Dreamstime.com, 107t Dreamstime.com/Olga Khoroshunova, 107cr Dreamstime.com/Franky, 108tr Dreamstime.com/memm74, 108b Dreamstime.com/Dennis Sabo, 109tr istockphoto.com, 109bl NOAA, 110tl istockphoto.com, 110b Dreamstime.com/Asther Lau choon siew, 111tl Dreamstime.com/Kwerry, 111r Dreamstime.com/Cornelis Opstal, 112-113 W. Perry Conway/CORBIS, 114t Dreamstime.com/Sergey Galushko , 114cl Tony Arruza/CORBIS, 114-115b Dreamsitme.com/Darren Baker, 115tr NOAA, 116b Dreamstime.com/John Wollwerth, 117tr NOAA, 117bl NOAA, 118t Dreamstime.com/Cathy Figuli, 118b Dreamstime.com/Nick Edens, 119tr Kip Evans, 119b Dreamstime.com/Alexei Novikov, 120-121 Dreamstime.com, 120bl Dreamstime.com/Brett Atkins, 121tr Dreamstime.com/Tommy Schultz, 121br istockphoto.com/David Safanda, 122tr Digital Vision, 122b Dreamstime.com/Roman Kazmin, 123t NOAA, 123cl Dreamstime.com/Steinar Figved, 124-125t Dreamstime.com/Inga Ivanova, 124bl Dreamstime.com/Asther Lau Choon Siew, 125cl Dreamstime.com/Asther Lau Choon Siew, 125bl istockphoto.com/Paul Topp, 126-127 Bob Gomel/CORBIS, 126cl istockphoto.com/Luis Carlos Torres, 127t NOAA, 127b Dreamstime.com/Roman Dekan, 128-129 Amos Nachoum/CORBIS, 128bl Dreamstime.com/Martin Strmko, 129br NOAA, 130t Digital Vision, 130b Dreamstime.com/Tommy Schultz, 131tr Digital Vision, 131b Dreamstime.com/David Lloyd, 132tr istockphoto.com/Kristian Sekulic, 132-133 Stuart Westmorland/CORBIS, 133t istockphoto.com, 134-135t Dreamstime.com/ Mikhail Blajenov, 135cr Uwe Kils, 135br Uwe Kils, 136cr NOAA, 137 Peter Herring/imagequestmarine.com, 137bl NOAA, 138-139 Ralph White/CORBIS, 140 Denis Scott/Corbis, 141t Dreamstime.com/Lenets Sergey, 141b NOAA, 142tr NOAA, 142b istockphoto.com/Charles Babbitt, 143tr NOAA, 144tr Dreamstime.com/Stephan Zabel, 144-145 Rick Price/CORBIS, 145br NOAA, 146tl Peter Parks/imagequestmarine.com, 146b NOAA, 148cl NOAA, 148tr NOAA, 148-149 Visuals Unlimited/Corbis, 149br New Zealand Ministry of Fisheries/Handout/epa/Corbis, 150tr USGS, 150b NOAA, 151t Dreamstime.com/Asther Lau Choon Siew, 152tr Stephen Frink/CORBIS, 153t NOAA, 154t NOAA, 154b NOAA, 155t Brandon D. Cole/CORBIS, 156tl NOAA, 156cr NOAA, 156br NOAA, 157tl Dreamstime.com/Jill Maroo, 157tr Dreamstime.com/Asther Lau Choon Siew, 157bl NOAA, 158bl NOAA, 159t Stuart Westmorland/CORBIS, 159cl NOAA, 160tl NOAA, 160bl NOAA, 161t NOAA, 161b NOAA, 162cl NOAA, 162b NOAA, 163tr NOAA, 163tc NOAA, 163cr NOAA, 164-165 Jenny E. Ross/Corbis, 166tl NASA, 166-167b Tim Davis/CORBIS, 167tr istockphoto.com, 167cl Dreamstime.com/Luke Pederson, 168t Dreamstime.com, 168bl Rick Price/CORBIS, 169tl NOAA, 169b Dreamstime.com/Natalia Bratslavsky, 170cr NASA, 170-171 Wolfgang Kaehler/CORBIS, 171br NOAA, 172tl istockphoto.com/John Pitcher, 172b istockphoto.com/Dmitry Deshevykh, 173 NOAA, 173cl Dreamstime.com/Kwerry, 174cl NOAA, 174-175 Rick Price/CORBIS, 175 NOAA, 175 NOAA, 176tl Dreamstime.com/Olga Solovei, 176-177 Dreamstime.com/Bernard Breton, 177tr istockphoto.com/Alexander Hafemann, 177br Dreametime.com/Vladimir Seliverstov, 178-179t Dreamstime.com/Jeff Goldman, 178bl istockphoto.com, 179tr Dreamstime.com/Vladimir Seliverstov, 179br Dreamstime.com/ Nikolay Alexandrov, 180tl istockphoto.com/Klaas Lingbeek van Kranen, 180b NOAA, 181t Dreamstime.com, 181bl NOAA, 182tr Dreamstime.com/Anthony Hathaway, 182b istockphoto.com/Stefan Klein, 183t Dreamstime.com/Gail Johnson, 183b istockphoto.com/John Pitcher, 184l Dreamstime.com/Vladimir Seliverstov, 184br Dreamstime.com/Oystein Sando, 185tl Paul Souders/Corbis, 185b istockphoto.com/Richard Waghorn, 186tl Dreamstime.com/Roy Longmuir, 186bl istockphoto.com/Roger Whiteway, 186-187 istockphoto.com/Mikhail Soldatenkov, 187tr Dreamstime.com/Aaron Whitney, 188tr Dreamstime.com/Andrew Buckin, 188-189b Roger Tidman/CORBIS, 189b NOAA, 190-191 Bettmann/CORBIS, 192-193 Natalie Fobes/CORBIS, 192b Dreamstime.com/Dragan Cvetanovic, 193tr istockphoto.com/John Peacock, 193cr istockphoto.com/Lim Weng Chai, 194cl Dreamstime.com/David Hyde, 194cr Dreamstime.com/Irochka, 194br istockphoto.com/Arne Thaysen, 194-195 Kevin Fleming/CORBIS, 195tr Chaiwat Subprasom/Reuters/Corbis, 195c istockphoto.com/Amanda Rohde, 196cl NOAA, 196-197 istockphoto.com/ Jan Kranendonk, 197tr Dreamstime.com/Kheng Guan Toh, 197br istockphoto.com/Willy Philippo, 198bl Dreamstime.com/Daniel Gale, 198-199 Stuart Westmorland/CORBIS, 199cr and br Dreametime.com/Joe Gough, 200tr NOAA, 200b Digital Vision, 201tr Chinch Gryniewicz; Ecoscene/CORBIS, 201l Digital Vision, 202-203t Dreamstime.com/Galina Barskaya, 202bl Digital Vision, 203cl Alan Schein Photography/CORBIS, 203cr istockphoto.com/Jonathan White, 204tl Jonathan Blair/CORBIS, 204br Stuart Westmorland/CORBIS, 205t Digital Vision, 205b NOAA, 206cr NOAA, 206br NOAA, 207tr Hulton-Deutsch Collection/CORBIS, 206-207b Jonathan Blair/CORBIS, 208t istockphoto.com/Harald Bolten, 208l Dreamstime.com/Vladimir Seliverstov, 209tr Dreamstime.com/ Tom Davison, 209br istockphoto.com, 210b Dreamstime.com/Asther Lau Choon Siew, 211tl Dreametime.com/Miguel Angelo Silva, 211tr NOAA, 211br NOAA, 212br courtesy of Wavegen, 212-213b istockphoto.com/Tore Johannesen, 213tl Dreametime.com/Uwe Ohse, 213tr Dreamstime.com/Fairn Whatley, 214tr Dreamstime.com/Alexander Putyata, 214b Dreametime.com, 215ct NOAA, 215tr Dreamstime.com/Paul Cowan, 215cl istockphoto.com/Jurga Rubinovaite.